ALSO BY PACO UNDERHILL

Why We Buy: The Science of Shopping

PACO UNDERHILL

CALL OF

THE MALL

SIMON & SCHUSTER • New York London Toronto Sydney

SIMON & SCHUSTER
Rockefeller Center
1230 Avenue of the Americas
New York, NY 10020

For information about special discounts for bulk purchases,
please contact Simon & Schuster Special Sales:
1-800-456-6798 or business@simonandschuster.com

Designed by Leslie Phillips

Manufactured in the United States of America

1   3   5   7   9   10   8   6   4   2

LIBRARY OF CONGRESS CATALOGING-IN-PUBLICATION DATA
Underhill, Paco.
Call of the mall / Paco Underhill.
p.   cm.
1. Shopping malls—United States.   2. Consumption (Economics)—United States.
3. Consumers—United States—Attitudes.   I. Title.
HF5430.3.U53   2004
306.3'0973—dc22   2003064960

ISBN 0-7432-3591-6

Generation 3 at Envirosell has been a good one.

Jenny Bonilla

Bob Bowman

Robyn Cushing

Diana Dawson

Kerry Elsasser

Gustavo Gomez

Dave Guerdette

Delise Dupont Jackson

Mark Pingol

Hillary Ross

Adrienne Sforza

Jennifer Vondrak

Contents

CALL OF THE MALL

Prologue

WHY ARE we here?
We're here to buy stuff.
We're here because we're bored.
We're here because tomorrow's Mother's Day.
We're here for the new Avril Lavigne CD.
We're here for emancipation.
We're here for lip gloss.
We're here because our mom made us come.
We're looking for sheets and towels.
We're looking for sex and love.
We're looking for self-esteem.
We're looking for jeans that fit.
We're here for our first business suit.
We're here because our daughter made us come.
We're here for a nice afternoon with the grandkids.
We're here for the food court.
We're here for the video arcade.
We're here for the movies.
We're here because it's pouring.
We're here to buy sneakers.
We're here because tomorrow's our anniversary.
We're here because he needs underwear.

1

We're here because she needs underwear.
We're here because everybody needs underwear.
We're here because there's nothing on TV.
We're here because it's fun!
We're here because our wife made us come.
We're here for no reason whatsoever.
We're looking for boys.
We're looking for girls.
We're looking for work.
We're looking to shoplift.
We're here because we love the mall!
We're here because everybody else is.
We're here because Christmas is coming.
We're here because Hanukkah is coming.
We're here because Kwanzaa is coming.
We don't know *why* we're here.
We're here to find . . . something.
We're here because *we're here*.

Introduction

ARE WE really going to spend an entire book inside a mall?

Yes, we are.

It's not as though studying people as they congregate to buy and sell things is a totally frivolous or small-minded endeavor. Consider the history of our species, a fair swath of which has been propelled by merchants or their emissaries traveling to the far reaches of the planet, sometimes at great risk, in order to bring back stuff to peddle to the rest of us. As any schoolchild can testify, the romance of the ancient world teems with spice routes and trade winds and trafficking in silks and precious metals, frankincense and myrrh, gunpowder and fur. Theoretically, we could all grow our own food and make our own clothes and build our own houses. But it would be boring. So let's agree that the saga of humankind can be told at least in part through the story of shopping.

Surely, then, you'll concur that the sites of so much significant social activity might be worth a look now and then? We tend to think of the mall as a recent, primarily American phenomenon, and a rather banal one at that, born of demographic convenience—we all bought cars and moved to the 'burbs—rather than any profound change in who or what we are. But the mall has been with us always, under other names and in somewhat different forms. Virtually since the dawn of civilization, we have organized our world in part around the function of shopping.

Even the simplest agrarian societies needed places to assemble to trade in goods, and from that basic impulse came everything else—marketplaces, villages, towns, cities. The mall is, at heart, just an ancient organizing principle that hasn't yet outlived its usefulness. Perhaps it never will.

But it's also easy to forget how recent the enclosed regional shopping mall is, maybe because it has so quickly become such a mainstay of American life. The first one popped up (in Edina, Minnesota) a mere seven decades ago, and now malls are the dominant arena of American shopping, which is itself an economic force the likes of which the world has never known. Without even meaning to, the mall has transformed our country, and not always for the good. For one thing, it drew shoppers away from vulnerable towns and big cities, and when that happened, decline usually set in. But there's no guarantee that malls will be with us forever. In fact, some evidence points to just the opposite outcome.

What's that, you say? You're okay with shopping but not with the mall? A common condition. Many otherwise fair-minded, intelligent people scorn and despise malls. Some still end up shopping in them on a regular basis. But they're not proud of it. You of this opinion may not be swayed by arguments of how the mall is a contemporary version of the souks, bazaars, arcades, bourses, and markets of olden days. But by studying the mall and what goes on there, we can learn quite a lot about ourselves—about the state of the nation and its inhabitants—from a variety of perspectives: economic, aesthetic, geographic, spiritual, emotional, psychological, sartorial.

I might agree with those who say that some of the adventure and romance associated with trading has been lost along the way. Somehow, the glorious history of commerce has culminated in a sanitized architectural cliché in which you typically find not exquisite treasures and exotic wares but rather eighty different styles of sneaker or sixteen varieties of chocolate chip cookie. No wonder we look at the mall—at the ambition of it, at the reality, at that already obese teenager stuffing her jaw with a drooling Cinnabon—and we can't help but wonder: Is this the best we could do?

It's no surprise that the mall is such an easy target for American self-loathing in particular. It's a lot like television in that way: another totally fake environment that attempts to pass itself off as a true reflection of who we are and what we want. We disdain it, and yet we can't stop watching. Or shopping. Once in a while, TV fulfills its highest calling—when a man first lands on the moon, say, or during the Watergate hearings. But most of the time it contents itself with reruns of *Three's Company* and infomercials for the home rotisserie.

It's the same with the mall. It *could* be much better—more vivid, intelligent, adventurous, entertaining, imaginative, alive with the human quest for art and beauty and truth. But it's not.

It's the mall.

1 *America Shops*

WE'RE DRIVING toward the mall.

I spend a lot of time in malls. Too much, I think. I daydream of life on a ranch out west where I'd go to Wal-Mart every two weeks for groceries, and that would be it for me and shopping.

It will never happen.

You are riding with a tall, bald, stuttering research wonk on the cusp of his fifty-third year. I am called a retail anthropologist, which makes me uncomfortable, especially around my colleagues still in academia who have many more degrees than I do. For whatever combination of reasons, I've spent my adult life studying people shopping. I watch how they move through stores and other commercial environments—restaurants, banks, fast-food joints, movie theaters, car dealerships, the post office, concert halls. Even in church, I study people. It is an odd skill, not one I would have sought. Yet I am good at it, and it pays the bills. I can't imagine not doing it.

I am definitely not a shopper. I don't own lots of stuff. When I do buy, in spite of whatever professional knowledge I have, I perform like an ordinary guy.

I own a research and consulting business called Envirosell. We work with merchants, marketers, and retail bankers around the world. Our specialty is looking at the interaction between people and products, and people and spaces. We look at all the ways in which retailers, product manufacturers, bankers, restaurateurs, and commercial and other public spaces either meet (or fail to meet) their customers' needs. It is a niche business, but it's our niche. We've been doing it for almost twenty years.

Our home office is in a funky landmark building, a former hotel, in New York City, in the middle of what was the department store district at the turn of the nineteenth century. We have an old-fashioned manual elevator run by a guy named Billy. The company occupies the hotel's second-floor lobby. I sit in the old manager's office, which has a gas fireplace I have never used. My south-facing windows look out onto what was once a Lord & Taylor store. It's now a shop that sells fancy dishes. We also have offices in Milan, São Paolo, Mexico City, Tokyo, Moscow, and Istanbul.

We have done hundreds of research jobs in mall stores. There are only six states of the fifty where we haven't worked a mall (the Dakotas, Alaska, Montana, Wyoming, and Louisiana). I average 130 days a year away from home, nearly all of which are spent in retail settings. I have been inside about three hundred North American malls, and some in other countries—Canada, Argentina, Brazil, Mexico, the United Arab Emirates, Italy, France, Spain, Holland, Germany, Sweden, Finland, Britain, Norway, Portugal, Turkey, Australia, Japan, Korea, Malaysia, Hong Kong; the list goes on and on. If someone mentions a mall somewhere in the United States—the Galleria in Houston, say, or the Del Amo in L.A.—I can picture the place, whether I want to or not. There are more than one hundred American malls to which I could give you accurate driving directions off the top of my head. I don't know whether to be proud or ashamed.

Okay, look around.

We're getting close to the mall, but you'd never know it. There are no directional signs anywhere on this highway, as there might be if we were headed toward Disney World or New York City or some other destination. The mall itself isn't a looming, dominating presence, even on this flat suburban landscape. We're just about to pass the only marker, a smallish road sign directing us to our exit, but beyond that there's nothing to steer us toward the mall, no attempt to inspire an impulse purchase, no billboard aimed at the road-weary traveler with an hour or two to kill. A mall is a huge commercial entity, but it tends to appeal strictly to the local shopper, the one who is already familiar with it and what it has to offer.

It's *our* mall. Maybe you have a mall, too.

You see a lot of a community's life in its mall. Families especially tend not to be on display in very many public spaces nowadays. You can find people in places of worship, but they tend to be on their best behavior, and they're mostly just standing or sitting. Increasingly, cities are becoming the province of the rich, the childless, or the poor. I love cities. But America hasn't lived there for a long time. The retail arena is still the best place I know for seeing what people wear and eat and look like, how they interact with their parents and friends and lovers and kids. If you really want to observe entire middle-class multigenerational American families, you have to go to the mall.

It's also not a bad place to shop.

A French historian I like named Daniel Roche wrote a book called *A History of Everyday Things.* In it, he examines and reconstructs the lives not of kings, queens, and generals but of ordinary French people in the seventeenth and eighteenth centuries—what they ate, what they wore, what they knew, and how they acquired what knowledge and possessions they had. In the spirit of Daniel Roche, this book is not about the official history of shopping malls and the tycoons who build and manage them. This is about malls, stores, and parking lots as experienced by us consumers.

Studying shopping provides the rhythm that governs my life—pack, leave home, fly somewhere, pick up a rental car, check into a hotel, then drive to a mall or store. For myself and my colleagues, it's a life of science and research, except instead of going to an excavation site in Peru, we end up at Tyson's Corner, a mall outside Washington, D.C. It's an unusual way to make a living, and an even odder way of experiencing and understanding a time and place.

On the other hand, I never run out of socks.

The job has become a habit. If I have two hours to kill before a flight out of Dallas, I'll visit the Irving Mall or Outdoor World on my way to the airport. I don't know what I expect to find; but like any research geek, I'm constantly on the lookout for something I haven't seen before—some innovation in digital signage, or a new sneaker style, or an interesting way to manage the line at the cash register. If I'm on vacation and get bored with the beach, I'll find the nearest mall and spend an afternoon there. It's not *such* a weird thing to do. If I said I enjoy a stroll along Madison Avenue in Manhattan, where Armani and Calvin and Donna Karan sit cheek by jowl, you'd understand. Doing it at the Beverly Center in Los Angeles or Bluewater outside London isn't so different.

I remember the first big research project my company landed, studying AT&T stores in two suburban Chicago malls. Back then it was just me and a few freelance researchers out in the field. Over a four-month period, we studied several incarnations of the same basic store, which meant I practically lived in those malls. I'd arrive at the telephone store and arrange the time-lapse cameras to watch how shoppers interacted with the merchandise and displays. The film cassettes had to be changed every two hours, so I couldn't stray too far, but unlike my researchers, I didn't have to remain inside the store. Moreover, I felt it was my responsibility not to appear in my own research footage. As a result, I spent many days roaming those malls—from ten A.M. to ten P.M. without a single productive thing to do except change film. I went into every store. I didn't buy much, but I saw a lot.

My fascination with stores is rooted in childhood. My father was a diplomat. As an offshore American raised in Third World nations and behind the Iron Curtain, my national identity was secondhand and based heavily on the Sears catalog. But to those around me, I was all-American. Sometimes I paid the price, like when I was beaten up on the street in Warsaw after the Bay of Pigs in 1961, or when rocks were thrown at our car in Seoul. When the kids in the British Army School I attended in Malaya chose sides for playground games, it often wound up as the few Americans against the rest of the world.

Still, to me America was always a far-off, mystical place, familiar yet completely exotic and fascinating. I wanted to feel connected to it, even long distance. When we'd return briefly to the States, I'd look at what the other kids were wearing, or playing with, or watching on TV, and realize how hopelessly out of it I was. It was painful to ask my grandmother to send me rock records, knowing that what she'd get would be awful, given her preference for Lawrence Welk. In Kuala Lumpur in 1963 there was no *American Bandstand* on TV, no T-shirts or lunch boxes. I was in cultural exile. My friend Steve was a little older than I and listened to a radio station he picked up from Bangkok. Thanks to him I knew that the Beatles existed, but that was about it.

Even today, that early cultural deprivation haunts my life. I am no good at the board game Trivial Pursuit, having missed too many cultural references from the 1960s and 1970s. I've had friends try to explain to me what was so hilarious about Rocky and Bullwinkle, or who the Waltons were, and why girls who favor Laura Ashley always liked *Little House on the Prairie*. I still don't get it.

Having gone from life abroad to living in downtown Manhattan, the shopping center was still an exotic locale, something I'd heard about but had little real exposure to. It's where, for the first time, I felt completely swallowed up inside white-bread middlebrow median-income America. It wasn't bad at all. I suddenly understood those 1980s émigrés from the Soviet Union who would come to this country and cry tears of joy over the splendor they found in the produce aisle of an average supermarket. At last I found what seemed to be the real America, and it was out shopping.

The morning of September 11, 2001, I was stranded in Dallas, unable to get home, which is a twenty-minute walk from what was the World Trade Center. On September 12 I spent the day wandering around the new mall in Plano, Texas. I just gravitated there. I needed to be around something familiar. It was the eeriest thing, though—a sparkling mall, in the middle of a beautiful September afternoon, with all the stores open and not a single shopper in the place. Around one-thirty I walked into a RadioShack and asked the clerk, "Am I the first person you've had in here today?"

"Yup," he said.

Strolling around got too lonely, so I decided to see a movie. I was just in time for *Tortilla Soup*. I was the only person in the theater. They screened it for me anyway. After the show I returned to my hotel, but I still had lots of time on my hands, so a few hours later I drove back to one of the mall's restaurants for dinner.

I was the only customer, but by the end of my meal the manager and the waiter had joined me at my table, and we three sat around drinking and talking, just the same as many people across the United States did that night. It felt all right to be doing it in a mall.

As I said before, I've devoted a lot of my life to malls, and in a few minutes we'll begin spending another Saturday in a typical one. We'll have lots of company.

Look up ahead—you *still* can't see it, but take my word, we're almost there.

2 *You Are Here*

ALMOST *where?*

We're going to spend today at a large regional enclosed mall, one of 1,175 in the United States at last count. Which specific mall we'll be visiting doesn't really matter, since the things we'll see and the lessons we'll learn apply to all. Therefore, I won't bother naming our destination, except to say it really does exist and it's a good one for our purposes.

But it's worth knowing a bit about the place and its history, since it *is* typical. This particular mall covers forty-six acres, including the parking lots. It is bordered and nourished by a six-lane state highway and a four-lane county road. We're in a suburb that's a twenty-minute drive (barring bad traffic) from a major metropolitan area. This is the largest mall in the immediate vicinity, although there is a slightly smaller one exactly four miles away. Both are owned by national commercial real estate development firms, companies with a history of ag-

13

gressive competition with one another. So a certain degree of rivalry exists between the malls, although both thrive. Perhaps that's because each has its own personality. Ours is known for its high-end stores. The other is more solidly middle class. Not low-rent by any means, but not haughty, either.

Early in the twentieth century, the land under our mall was the estate of a wealthy local family. By the mid-twentieth century, the fortune and family were gone, and the plot was vacant. A developer bought it in the early 1950s and built a department store on the site. A decade or so later, some smaller stores were added around it, creating an ad hoc open-air shopping center. Three decades ago, a second department store was built on this parcel. Not long after, the developer announced plans to enclose the entire development under one roof—to turn it into a proper mall. It was an easy decision to make: In the early 1970s, *U.S. News & World Report* conducted a poll and found that adult Americans spent more time at malls than anywhere else except for home and work. This was in the feverish early stage of our love affair with malls, back when a few new ones opened every week and no suburb felt complete without at least one.

Turning the shopping center here into a mall involved a major construction project that went on while the existing stores remained open for business. Today, total gross leasable area in the complex is nearly 1.5 million square feet, which puts it among the top 2 or 3 percent of American malls—big, in other words, though still considerably smaller than the largest mall in North America (Canada's Edmonton Mall, over 5 million square feet) or the United States (Mall of America, in Bloomington, Minnesota, over 4 million square feet).

Our mall reeks of money—inside we'll see acres of marble, in tasteful shades of tan, brown, and white. The flooring is tile. There's a glassed-in elevator. There are 144 stores. Befitting its middle- to upper-middle-class market, there's a Versace and a Ralph Lauren, a Cartier and a Tiffany, a Nordstrom and a Saks. There's also a Gap, an Abercrombie & Fitch, a Victoria's Secret, but no Spencer Gifts. The biggest single category is women's apparel, which is also the mainstay of every other mall in the world. There's a record store, a toy store, a video game store and nine stores selling sneakers. There must be close to twenty places to buy cosmetics, if you include the department stores and the boutiques that sell it as a sideline. There's a beauty parlor with big, old-fashioned hair dryers that look like something out of a science-fiction movie.

There's also a fourteen-screen cinema at which, this weekend, two screens are devoted to the new Jackie Chan movie. (I can't wait.) There's a video arcade. There's a rock-climbing wall. There's an Aqua Massage, which requires more explanation than I can pause for here. (But maybe we'll give it a whirl later.) There are three national chain sit-down restaurants, all civilized affairs, serving food that's utterly acceptable. There's a food court, a vast, high-ceilinged arena offering no fewer than forty different outlets, mostly fast food. There's a funny little 1950s-style hamburger joint, Johnny Rockets, in which the waitstaff, a bunch of listless teenagers in dingy uniforms, are required to perform a line dance several times an hour. It's hilarious and distressing, and I recommend it highly. There's a Cinnabon stand, four cookie stands, three pretzel stands, three ice-cream stands, and no place wheresoever to buy an apple.

There's no bookstore, hardware store, home electronics store, computer store, sporting goods store, or office supply store. Perhaps not coincidentally, all these categories of retail typically attract a high proportion of adult male shoppers. There are not very many adult males here except for those in the company of women or children.

Usually, malls this size draw shoppers from between five and twenty-five miles away. According to one survey, 30 percent of the adults living in this county have been here at least once during the past three months. Just 2 percent of adults living in the two neighboring counties visited during the same span.

Today, malls account for around 14 percent of all U.S. retailing (not counting cars or gasoline), about $308 billion in annual sales. Our mall accounts for just over $600 million in sales a year. It's our duty as Americans to add to that. So let's get going.

3 A Mouse Hole

FEAST your eyes.

It's big and beige and boxy. Virtually featureless. What else could it be? We're here.

The first glimpse of any mall is usually also a look at what's wrong with mall architecture in general. From the outside, as a rule, malls give us no clear idea of what's inside. This is not a good thing.

Little consideration seems to have been given to how the building will appear to the shopper as he or she approaches from the highway. No one has bothered to create something that says *shopping*, let alone says it clearly or handsomely or interestingly. The ugliness of much of roadside America is discouraging, and malls are the largest buildings ever dedicated to the art of retailing in the history of the planet. So their ungainliness is of monumental stature and gargantuan scale.

It's no great mystery why this should be so.

For centuries, the people who built places to shop tended to be merchants. And so they took seriously their responsibility to attract shoppers. They created environments intended to present their wares, and to give shoppers a sense of moment, of event, of *place*. You can look back to the ancient Greek *storas* or the bazaars and souks in the days before Christ and find a merchant aesthetic already at work. A selling space didn't have to be fancy or pretty, and it didn't need to be built from luxurious materials. In many cases, just the opposite was true—an environment where goods are sold at rock-bottom prices *should* feel authentically no-frills. If you're interested in fresh vegetables and fruit, nothing is more promising than a rough-hewn roadside stand or rustic farmer's market. You wouldn't want your neighborhood newsstand to feel like a fancy jewelry shop, and you don't want a lumberyard to look like a florist. In each instance, the design of the store itself is a reflection of the main activity taking place within.

Look around any American city that still sports prewar architecture, and you may find at least a few grand emporiums of the past, the department store. In many places, New York included, some examples continue to stand: Bloomingdale's, Saks, Lord & Taylor. The principles of good retailing held sway everywhere, starting with the architecture. The buying experience began when you, the shopper, first caught sight of the edifice. It got the acquisitive juices flowing.

There was another force at work, too. The merchant princes were nineteenth century men, driven by ambition and muscle and determination to succeed in the brick-and-mortar vocabulary of the era. Their stores were their alter egos, and these titans of retailing all had serious edifice complexes. The great department stores of the day bore their owners' names—Gimbel, Macy, Wanamaker, Neiman Marcus, Marshall Field. These men were the contemporaries of figures like David Rockefeller and Andrew Carnegie, captains of industry who left their lasting marks on the world. Bank buildings were temples to one impulse, and city halls to another, and stores to yet another. Today, public architecture still expresses intentions and functions: sports arenas, libraries, hotels, universities—their design usually attempts to articulate something about what goes on inside. At the very least, they manage to look different from one another.

But then there are malls.

In part, their inglorious history is to blame. The mall was begat by the shopping center, which was begat by the humble little strip of stores facing a parking lot, which was the first form of shopping begat by suburbia. The earliest retail organization principle inspired by automotive life was that strip of shops—sometimes anchored by a supermarket—featuring maybe six or eight little establishments. There would be a row of parking spots out front, and easy zoom-in zoom-out access off the road. The shopping center's innovation was to turn things around, so that the stores faced not the road but one another—a circling of the suburban wagons, so to speak, now surrounded by (rather than facing) the parking spots. It was a small step from there to placing a roof over the whole thing. That history, and the fateful turning away from the eyes of the outside world, steered the mall to the state in which we find it.

Today's malls do a dismal job of signaling us as to what goes on inside. This is mainly because of the disconnect that exists at their very core. Malls house retailing, but they are not owned, developed, or built by retailers. Malls are made by real estate development companies. The men who direct these firms are not merchant princes. They are the ones who take the risk—who amass the parcel of land, line up the financing, secure all the governmental permits, and then hire the architects and contractors and so on. But they make money by putting space to work. Their tools of the trade are a spreadsheet and a good leasing agent. The mandate is to turn a hunk of suburban turf into a gold mine, something that generates profits by charging rents and a percentage of the take, not by peddling goods or services. It's very different from the financial model of their tenants, the stores. The mall exists to contain stores—it is, in fact, a store of stores. But it does not think of itself as a store. That is at the heart of what's lacking about malls, and, through the course of this book, it will come up over and over again.

Anyway, here we are. What do we see?

"A big wall with a little mouse hole" is how typical exterior mall architecture was described to me—and this was by the design director of one of America's biggest and most respected mall developers. If even his firm was willing to settle for that usual configuration of high blank walls punctuated by nondescript entrances, it's no wonder that most malls are eyesores, at least from the outside. Aesthetic value is the last thing on anyone's mind when imagining a mall.

That's a problem.

The fact that some malls are well designed just explains why most are not. Typically, city malls possess some design equity. They look good. I'm thinking of Faneuil Hall, in Boston, one of the handsomest landmarks in that city. It was made to look good in part because its developer knew that it would be a showpiece. Everybody who comes to Boston eventually visits. Another reason urban malls tend to be well designed is that city governments are adept at forcing real estate developers to build things with intrinsic value that enhance their surroundings. Municipal lawyers, planners, and community and design review boards are experienced at hammering out compromises that, in the end, benefit all parties. As a result, urban malls usually are made to fit harmoniously with their surroundings. This is true in cities all over the world. Lisbon, Portugal, is home to one of the world's most striking malls, the Vasco da Gama Center, which was built to look like a giant ship. Diagonal Mar, in Barcelona, Spain, also manages to make a mall a beautiful thing. Bluewater, in Great Britain, used to be a quarry; in Atlanta, a defunct steel mill and notorious brownsite is being turned into Atlantic Station, a New Urbanist development built to integrate housing, offices, and shopping. So it's possible for shopping centers even to improve on what they replace.

But imagine what typically happens when a big developer makes its intentions known to a suburban township. Most local governments have little experience at hammering out these deals, since most suburbs get only a few such projects in a lifetime. Even if the township wanted to play hardball and force the developer to spend money on a handsome design, or one with extra features such as parks or community centers, the mall owner holds all the cards. It's easy enough to move the mall a few miles away, within another town's boundaries. Now consider the extent to which a shopping center will contribute to a suburb's tax coffers—a big regional mall can easily cover most of what it takes to run a township school system. It's hard to say no over a question of architectural integrity.

Mall of America, the biggest in the United States and the most potent tourist attraction in all of Minnesota, may have looked good on the drawing board. But it has aged badly since it opened in August 1992. You can see stains on the outside of the building, and grass has begun to poke through the asphalt of the parking lots. It is huge and unsightly. You can't imagine Disney World or the Statue of Liberty being allowed to decay this way. Yet this mall has more visitors than Disney World, Graceland, and the Grand Canyon combined.

Next time you're at a mall, instead of going directly inside, stroll around the perimeter of the place. It will be one of the more joyless promenades you'll ever make. You'll be very alone out there, on a narrow strip of sidewalk, assuming it has a sidewalk—many malls don't—with maybe a security guard or two to keep you company. (They'll be watching you closely, since someone who walks around a mall is, by definition, an odd character.) There will almost certainly be shrubbery, neatly clipped, but it's greenery of the most generic kind. Nobody thought you'd ever look too closely at it. Its only job is to be green.

The building itself may be in good condition, depending on its age and the quality of materials used, but still the surface might be chipped, cracked, or discolored. Nobody takes this stuff too seriously, since nobody ever thought you'd be walking out here to notice. You'll no doubt come upon America's new pariah class, smokers. They'll be gathered by the entrances, close to the industrial-size ashtrays. There may be an occasional cell phone caller out there, too, in search of optimal reception.

Some malls feature display windows facing the parking lots, and some don't. Windows are problematic in a setting such as this because there's no real pedestrian approach to the building. You may drive up close to it while searching for a parking spot, but if you decide to examine the store windows you'll crash your car. Once you've parked, you dash to your destination: inside. Maybe it's raining or it's cold. It could easily be windy, given the lack of any neighboring structures. And anyway, you're here to walk around a mall, not a parking lot. A store may have the most spellbinding windows in the world, but nobody is going to pay much attention in a mall parking lot. All the action is on the inside.

Fashion Show, the ultra-glitzy mall in Las Vegas, exhibits a unique flair for architecture and visual presentation starting on the outside. It's one of the splendors of the Strip, which is saying something. Signage technology gets more spectacular every day—take a walk through Times Square in New York, a magnet for tourists from around the world, and you witness all manner of digital video, huge-screen TVs, vividly colored "ribbons" of news headlines slithering at high speed around curvilinear building facades. These same innovations exist at every sports stadium and rock concert hall—we're a nation of cutting-edge sophisticates where big visual communication technology is concerned. Our eyes are trained to watch for the next hot thing.

Of course, it's impossible to prove that more attention to architecture would make a bit of difference to a mall's bottom line. In the end, that argument carries the day—the marketplace doesn't require more beautiful shopping center design, so why spend more for it? That's the short view, at least. Today, when most American malls are over twenty years old, the question of what to do about aging centers will soon be upon us. If the buildings themselves had any intrinsic value, we'd be more likely to restore or salvage ones that need it. We restore and re-purpose many public structures, such as former post offices, hotels, libraries, even churches. But most malls are too ugly and banal to warrant such effort. They've been designed to be serviceable, nothing more, and once they no longer can serve they'll have to be razed, and replaced with . . . I don't know. Maybe something even worse.

We need to find a place to park.

4 Dude, Where's My Car?

OKAY, NOW we're *really* here. Nearly really here, I should say. We still have to park.

Because America lives by the automobile, we live by the parking space, too. When ruminating over all the reasons that city dwellers embraced suburbia, we sometimes overlook the promise of painless parking. Imagine the daily ordeal of primitive man circa 1950, back when urban streets designed for horse and wagon traffic became home to two- and three-car baby boom families. The lure of knowing that you could retire from the nightly blood sport of parallel parking, never again to circle endlessly while waiting for another driver to budge, was part of what inspired urban flight. Not only racial unease or class aspirations. Pure convenience. Having a garage or just a driveway of one's own was bliss.

Try to imagine any suburban institution such as the mall without parking. Can't be done.

The entrance to the parking lot is where the mall really begins. As you approach, there's always that moment of anticipation when you see whether the lot is full, empty, or somewhere in between. It sets the tone for the day. Enjoy a smooth transition from the highway to the front door, and you feel blessed. Hit a snag, and you start your shopping trip under a black cloud.

Once in the lot, you could drive around and around the building without ever finding an entrance that announces itself as the "main" one. There may be several unprepossessing doorways at regular intervals, none of them marked with any kind of sign to alert you to what lies inside. Or, you may just take the easy way out and enter through one of the department stores. Even if there is one mall entrance that feels like a primary one, this may not be the one used by all or even most shoppers. We've studied many malls where there *is* one door used by people unfamiliar with the mall. We call it the "stranger" entrance. But it's usually not the portal of choice for those who know the mall well.

In fact, mall design reflects the same lack of hierarchy of which suburbs themselves are often guilty. Cities organize themselves into distinct zones—downtown, outskirts, central business district, rich-people housing, middle-class housing, poor-people housing, good part of town, bad part of town, and so on. This scheme has evolved over the course of centuries, and so we're all familiar with it the instant we come upon it.

Suburbs are to a large degree an escape from that urban structure—they are islands of homes with enough retail to serve most of the natives' needs, and then just enough institutional uses (schools, police stations, firehouses, churches, movie theaters) to get along. The mall reflects that lack of hierarchy. A single main entrance would run counter to the suburban automotive ideal, which dictates that you should always be able to park as close as possible to your own personal destination. So, instead of the most desirable parking spots being concentrated in one area, they form a ring around the building. Your parking priorities will almost certainly differ from mine. It permits a truly American freedom of choice, expressed in a form of architectural and spatial chaos.

When choosing a mall parking spot, you've got four priorities to juggle:

1. You want a spot that's easy and fast to reach when you arrive.
2. You want a spot close to the mall.
3. You want a spot near the entrance that will bring you closest to your first destination inside.
4. You want a spot that's fast and easy to reach when you leave.

Parking within fifty feet of your preferred entrance is probably the highest priority of the four, especially when it's cold, hot, or rainy, but even when it's nice outside. Nobody enjoys a springtime stroll through a mall parking lot. When you shop in a city, getting to your destination is an enjoyable part of the experience and may turn up some pleasant surprises along the way. All manner of information is gleaned, almost without noticing, when we walk down a city street. We see other store windows, of course, but also we get to study how people dress, how they wear their hair, what kind of dogs they walk. None of that exists in the parking lot of a mall.

I've spent plenty of time out here in the lot, and not just in my car. Often, when I start a consulting assignment for a retail chain or developer, I'll drag executives out here. They're usually puzzled: *Wait a sec—the stores are in there!* But I insist. For all their knowledge and experience, few merchants or managers understand how much of the customer experience takes place in the parking lot. Executives who would be appalled by a lack of regard for shopper comfort within the store don't give a moment's thought to what happens out here.

"Can't we just go into the security office and see the lot on the video monitor?" I've been asked.

"Not the same," I say.

So we all trudge out there. I march my captives to the farthest extreme of the lot, and then make them stand there a minute. Part of my mission is to get them to see the mall itself as the shopper first encounters it. I want them to witness how the signage and display windows play under normal conditions.

If the mall devoted much thought to how shoppers experience the place, they'd spend a little money and effort on the parking lot. As soon as you turned in off the road you'd come upon a car greeter—a traffic cop. He'd be the boss, and he would have two or three minimum-wage high school kids running around to inform drivers where all the spots are, would keep traffic moving smoothly, and would give shoppers the sense that fairness and order prevail.

Doesn't happen. I've been at this particular mall on the Saturday before Christmas when by ten A.M. traffic is at a standstill and tempers are flaring. Mall management remains uninvolved. Find your own spot, fight your own battles, it tells us, *then* come inside. Mall operators think they control parking lots by installing surveillance cameras. As any police officer will tell you, control is about being visible. Most of the time this isn't a huge issue, but there are about thirty shopping days a year when this lot will reach capacity. On those days, a little help would go a long way.

*   *   *

We all have our own personal parking styles—it's just one more way we express who we are. Some philosophical types are content to park at the farthest reaches of the lot and trudge in from there; more competitive drivers will stalk the prime spots, even tailing shoppers as they exit the mall and head to their cars. I had an aunt who refused to park where she had to back out.

There's also the matter of how we will find our cars when it's time to leave. How many of us pay only half attention to the landmarks of the lot? Research has shown that people landmark the lot based on age and gender. Men like numbers and letters. Women like colors. Kids prefer symbols—animals or fruit. For every time I've memorized my landmarks, there have been more where I have wandered aimlessly looking for my chariot. On those days I walk row after row of cars pressing my keyless ignition, muttering, "Here, Greta [the name I've given my Audi], where *are* you?" At a mall outside Houston, after an hour of searching for my rental, I began to doubt my sanity. I missed my flight that day. There must be some kind of car homing device that Hertz could install. That little gizmo would win my loyalty forever.

*   *   *

Malls treat parking lots as necessary evils. I wish developers would notice how we sometimes make great, creative use of these broad expanses of asphalt. The obvious example is something most sports fans are familiar with—tailgating parties and picnics in the stadium parking lot. Some of these efforts are downright lavish, with charcoal grills and Champagne coolers set up amid campers, minivans, and trailers. Ford now makes a truck with optional sink and gas grill.

That marriage of RV camping and parking lot has been handsomely exploited by Wal-Mart. To the horror of campground owners across the United States, the giant retailer now permits overnight camper parking in its lots. This is a genius move—the overnighters take advantage of the stores' bathrooms in the morning, but those folks also spend money on food, clothing, and supplies. The NASCAR circuit has reinvented another ancient retail tradition—the peddler's wagon. On race days, trailers park in the lot and turn into stores with varied product lines that put the old factory parking lot "roach coach" (my favorite term for lunch wagons) to shame.

The concept of the portable open-air store has merit. The best example I know is the tent sale that happens in the high-end carpet business. Bloomingdale's Home Store and others use it to good advantage. The huge tent goes up in a parking lot, carpets are piled inside, and for an intense week or two the store conducts what ends up being a huge percentage of its annual rug business. It shows that under the right conditions you can sell even a very fine and costly product in a parking lot.

Some supermarkets are great utilizers of the parking lot. In summer, you'll find a little convenience store set up out there, maybe under a tent to protect the cashier from sunstroke. They don't stock the usual C-store items such as milk, beer, and aspirin. Instead you'll find bags of charcoal briquettes, barbeque tools, lawn chairs, sun hats, water guns, bug spray, suntan lotion, and other trappings of suburban summer. This is the stuff you always remember only at the last minute, and the market saves you the trouble of running back through the entire store to pick up a few Saturday afternoon essentials. If you came to the market with no intention of buying any of that stuff, the ministore out front is a potent reminder.

What frustrates me as a researcher is that parking lot innovations are being tried, but on an ad hoc basis, with no attempt to measure what works and what does not. As small-town main streets have died, the biggest and most predictable public gathering in many communities is the big shopping center parking lot. That's a phenomenon to be taken advantage of, not ignored or discouraged.

A few years ago I was part of a small group hired to help the Phoenix Zoo imagine its future. The director picked us up at the hotel in the zoo's minivan, covered with airbrushed animals rendered in bright colors. As we pulled into the parking lot, he drove toward his spot, closest to the main entrance. I asked him to park instead in the middle of the empty lot. As we walked away, two cars screeched to a stop and a bunch of young boys ran to examine the van up close.

"If you have a billboard," I told the director, "use it."

A common problem in all suburban shopping used to be when employees arrived early and hogged all the best parking spots. By now, most stores recognize this and order staffers to park away from the front door. Rarely, the problem is just the opposite. Recently my firm studied something found only in rural America—the Farm & Fleet network. These regional chains run huge stores—a hundred thousand square feet and up—that serve farmers and rural businesses. They stock an enormous cross section of goods, from jeans and high-end cowboy boots to barbed wire and harnesses for your donkey. Out on the edges of nowhere, these stores sit in the middle of endless parking lots. Rural land is still cheap.

The problem is that the lots often look painfully empty. The store we studied required employees to park behind the store. As a result, when you drove by in the morning, the lot was deserted, and you couldn't be sure the store was open. Our advice was to move employee parking around to the front, midway through the lot—thereby leaving the prime spots for shoppers, but signaling to passing drivers that the store was open for business.

Hey! How's this spot? It's near a fairly nondescript entrance to the mall, a fine place through which to enter the belly of the beast. Help me remember where we are: E6, E6, E6, let's go, E6.

5 Why Malls Fear Freedom

WHAT HAVE we here? It looks to be three hundred or so six-year-olds assembled in an open space on the mall's ground floor, just inside the entrance, kicking at one another as hard as they can. Their mothers and fathers and siblings surround the squalling mob, smiling and waving. How wholesome can you get?

All over American malldom, similar scenes are playing out—here we see the local martial arts schools raising money for a worthy cause with what they call a "kick-a-thon." Somewhere else, it's the local ballet school, or the glee club, the marching band, the Boy Scouts, the art league, the roller hockey league, the Junior League, the spelling bee, the high school drama club performing highlights from *Brigadoon*. Or is that *Bye Bye Birdie*?

This is where the mall-as-community shows its shiny, peppy face. If we were a village society, or even an urban one, these activities might take place at the schoolhouse, or the community center, or in the vil-

29

lage green on market day. But since we're a predominately suburban nation, and suburbs tend to be short on gathering places, it all happens at the mall.

For which the mall, of course, is mostly happy. It's not earning a profit on every kick these little tae kwon do apostles deliver, but this is a good way to ensure the presence of their moms and dads at ten-thirty on a Saturday morning. Once you've gone to all the effort of driving here and parking, it seems wasteful not to acquire something or other. Best of all, the little ones may be so exhausted by then that they'll behave themselves. The mall likes having the cute children of wage-earning parents around. It brightens up the place. It's cheaper than real entertainment. It's good for the image. There's a profit motive to being such a willing host and accommodator of various community-minded endeavors.

Some of the attempts by suburbanites to take seriously the mall as quasi-public space seemed innocuous enough. For example, an entirely new form of mass exercise was born of the mall. No sooner had America's first enclosed shopping center opened, in 1956, in the Minneapolis suburb of Edina, than did area doctors begin advising older patients to get their cardiovascular exercise inside the mall, where they could stride without fear of slipping on snow or ice. Mall walking quickly caught on. If you've ever gone into a mall before the stores open (as I have), you know the sound—the silence is broken only by the squeak of senior citizen mall walkers in their sneakers. Many malls decided to extend a special welcome to these elders in sweat suits and began allowing them inside before normal business hours. (There was always the chance that they'd stick around and buy something.) Some shopping centers began special programs for senior citizens—mall-walker clubs, free coffee, discount coupons, holiday parties.

And then, inevitably, came the backlash. Malls began to feel taken advantage of by the walkers, some of whom began to feel entitled to the amenities and special favors they had been granted. There was always some question as to whether the discounts and programs actually made any economic sense. Eventually, some developers tried curtailing mall walking altogether. Mall of America attempted to force mall walkers to use a parking lot so far from the building that shuttle buses were required. The walkers retaliated with an informational campaign, reminding the stores of how much money they spent there. Before long the mall caved in and allowed normal parking for all.

More recently, Evergreen Plaza, near Chicago, attempted similar measures. Management aired its grievances in the local press, complaining about senior citizen sneakers muddying newly polished floors, and mall walkers hogging all the good parking spots and demanding Christmas gifts. "It got out of control from a standpoint of entitlement," a mall executive told a reporter. "Predominately they are seniors, okay, and seniors are not great spenders, are they?" Perhaps not, but they excel at gaining public sympathy in battles such as this one. A torrent of bad publicity ensued, reaching all the way to page one of the *New York Times*. Competing malls even began making a play for the banished senior citizens, at which point Evergreen Plaza management turned tail and invited the walkers back.

"Mall walking is pretty much a given and something that is hard for malls to avoid," a spokesperson for a mall developer trade group said in an article. "On the whole, our industry embraces the walkers as viable customers. The rub some retailers might have is that they tend to get there early and take the best parking spots. And they are not really that dynamic as shoppers."

Sneaker-scuffed floors are the least of the inconveniences that come with being suburban functional Main Streets, malls have learned. The various free speech–related activities that go with American democracy soon followed everyone else to the mall—the activists realized there was no other way to be encountered in a suburban milieu where no one walks. These were the moments that tried a mall's commitment to a vision of itself as some kind of quasi-public space, the town center for towns where no true center exists. This got at the heart of the question of whether a mall is the suburban Main Street or a tightly controlled fortress devoted to a single activity: retailing. Or is it somewhere in between?

Political candidates collecting signatures, activists protesting, sympathizers leafleting for causes popular and otherwise, even Klansmen, all descended upon American malls. In 1968, the U.S. Supreme Court began getting involved in the matter. In that year, it ruled that malls cannot interfere with the exercise of First Amendment rights. Score one for the people. Then, four years later, it reversed itself and said the First Amendment did not require shopping centers to permit the distribution of antiwar leaflets on the premises. Score one for the mall. That ruling seemed to settle the argument by establishing shopping centers as private property, the same as an individual store might be.

Then, in 1980, in a unanimous decision involving a California mall, the court said that individual states' laws could require malls to allow greater free-speech rights than the First Amendment does. Since then, courts in six states (California, Colorado, Massachusetts, New Jersey, Oregon, and Washington) have deemed malls to be at least quasi-public spaces, where at least some forms of expressions must be allowed. Eleven more—Arizona, Connecticut, Georgia, Michigan, Minnesota, New York, North Carolina, Ohio, Pennsylvania, South Carolina, and Wisconsin—have decided not to require malls to behave like public places.

*   *   *

Developers are technically correct when they point out that the mall is private property, not the village square. According to one survey, nearly three-quarters of shoppers believe the mall *should* keep out political activists—which is consistent with what we know of the average person's tolerance for commotion (especially when it interferes with shopping). And yet, the fact is that the mall phenomenon came along and took the place of the town square, the public zone.

The mall is a monument to the moment when Americans turned their back on the city. To many of us, cities are civilization's greatest achievement—they are vast, complicated, marvelous machines created by our collective energies and dreams, a way for us to come together to live, work, play, love, learn, create, protest, worship, and die, all in one glorious place. Cities, going back to Athens, managed to bring together every imaginable worthwhile human activity (and some not so worthwhile ones) in harmonious fashion. A good city—hell, a good city block—is a treasure forever. I've gotten myself in trouble for saying that America's villains of the twentieth century were Frank Lloyd Wright for romanticizing the suburbs and Henry Ford for making the suburban dream accessible. To be fair, many of the cities people fled were dangerous, dirty, and unhealthy. The trade-off in quality-of-life terms was probably a good one. This book is about one consequence of that flight: a big air-conditioned vanilla box with all the action on the inside.

If you need proof of suburban malls' smug, insular nature, consider this: They can almost never be easily reached by public transportation. If you can't drive here, the mall seems to say, you can't come. This is in marked contrast to European and Japanese malls, which are often built near train stations for the convenience of shoppers. In Japan, malls even feature bicycle racks, something I've never seen in the United States, although a great many people live within bike distance of malls and might like the chance to get a little fresh air and exercise in with their shopping.

America's postwar suburbs are for the most part inhospitable to *any* form of transportation that isn't an automobile. So the mall isn't remarkable in this regard. But sometimes the consequences are tragic. In 1995, an African American teenager was killed while trying to cross a busy seven-lane highway on her way to a mall near Buffalo, New York. She was forced to walk across the road because the mall prohibited city buses from stopping on the property. Local civil rights activists accused the developer of doing so in order to keep out minorities, since the buses carried residents from a mostly black part of town. The mall denied any racial motive, saying it wanted only to keep rowdy young people away. The bus ban was lifted after the activists threatened a boycott. The dead girl's family sued the mall, which settled the case for $2 million.

Are malls racist? It's not such an outlandish question. It seems clear that malls hope by limiting public transportation they can control who may enter and who may not. The fact that you need to drive doesn't completely ensure that a mall will get only the law-abiding middle class, since in America people of extremely modest means still manage to own cars. Still, city dwellers and teenagers most often are the ones without wheels. So keeping the mall unattainable by public transportation goes a long way toward segregating it from anything even potentially scary.

Malls might argue that, from a business point of view, keeping low-income urban teenagers out is a smart goal. In one survey, 50 percent of malls claimed they had problems with gangbangers, and 90 percent said they had attracted troublesome teenage loiterers. After all, the mall is meant to be a refuge from the bad city streets, from cold and wind and rain but also from panhandlers and vagrants and teenagers with bad attitudes.

In truth, it's easy to stroll these tranquil pathways and forget that crime exists anywhere, let alone that shopping districts are sometimes magnets for pickpockets, shoplifters, and muggers. That's the lulling effect of the mall—you are surrounded only by fellow shoppers, all drawn together in a communion of consumption. There are no outskirts here, no dark recesses or easy getaway routes (not even for the law-abiding), which makes crimes such as purse snatching an unlikely occurrence.

Suburban subdivisions segregate people based on how much they can spend on real estate. Everybody knows that wealth and poverty exist, but many suburbanites get no closer to either end of the spectrum than their television screen. We humans seem to find comfort in economic homogeneity, and the mall does its best to preserve that condition.

We are living in a time when, nationally, crime is down, especially the personal, violent offenses that worry us most—murder, robbery, rape, and assault. The danger of urban streets, whether real or presumed, is part of what drove us to the suburbs and then to the mall in the first place.

I know a mall in a posh suburb of New York that was a target for organized urban criminals. A few years ago, police reported that a modern-day Fagin was actively recruiting city teenagers to plunder the place as shoplifters and pickpockets. In one day more than forty youths were arrested while shoplifting there. In all, more than one hundred arrests were made, including children as young as eleven. Some were discovered with printed manuals telling them which bus routes would get them to the mall, and then which stores to hit once they got there. The guides instructed them in the art of hiding their loot, evading guards, and exiting the mall swiftly; the kids knew which designers' clothes could be most easily fenced once they got it home. At the Mall of America there have been a few shootings and some assaults, all attributed to gangs. There has been one murder (of a seventeen-year-old woman, by her estranged boyfriend). There were also a few rapes, including one of a teenage girl, in a service corridor, by a man she had met at the mall that day.

Malls probably don't need to make much special effort to keep dangerous elements out. There's already a remarkably efficient self-regulating mechanism that maintains orderliness in the world of shopping. It uses symbolism and nuance to attract certain people while repelling certain others. Say what you will about the snootiest shopping districts of any city in America—you can get there by public transportation, or even on foot, no matter where you live. In New York, for instance, it takes only subway fare to go from some of the poorest, toughest neighborhoods in the city—indeed, the country—to some of the poshest, most exclusive boutiques in the world. There's no obvious police or private security presence stopping armed thugs or mobs of marauding adolescents from descending upon Madison Avenue and making waste of it. And yet, it doesn't happen.

People of modest means may dream of someday indulging a taste for Armani, but they tend not to try for it until they can afford it, and no armed guard is required to turn them away in the meantime. People enjoy shopping in places where they feel wanted and needed and loved, even people without much money. They have their own favorite stores where they shop, not necessarily out of need but because it's fun. Even muggers and stick-up men take their ill-gotten gains and go shopping like everybody else.

We think of malls as being wholesome and all-American, but they are not uniformly so. Some are also snobbish, xenophobic, elitist. Hateful. But we're *still* going to spend the day here.

6 *I Brake for Meanderthals*

SPEAKING of mall walking, how are you holding up? Strolling around in here is quite a bit easier than doing it in a city. For one thing, there's no weather to worry about. For another, the pace is quite a bit slower. This is one of the areas in which, almost undetected, the mall has had a huge effect on American life: it has actually taught us to walk differently than we once did, as we'll see. Huge deal, right? That's especially so for me, since in my line of work the way people walk has major implications for how they shop. We now have several generations of Americans who have never walked for any length of time in cities or even towns. They ride everywhere and walk only here, at the mall. Which is quite a bit different from walking anywhere else.

For safety's sake, you maintain your gaze at eye level and under when walking city streets. In New York City, a pedestrian walking briskly covers about three hundred feet per minute. As you move, your eyes do, too, shifting slightly from side to side covering almost a full

180-degree semicircle. As human eyes age, depth perception deterio-
rates, and we put less trust in our peripheral vision. An older person is
much more conscious of where her feet are. Children tend to move
their heads more than adults do; in our research work, eight-year-olds
are the ones who spot our cameras, never teens or adults. Head position while walking in a city is also a matter of preference; people would
rather look at other people than just about anything else.

Nevertheless, you're also on the lookout for the usual pedestrian
hazards, such as curbs, potholes, and homeless people lying in nooks
and crannies. But with the advent of traffic lights and good paving,
urban eyes are usually earthbound. From the retailer perspective, this
is good—it keeps our eyes more or less in the zone of store window displays.

These conditions do not allow city walkers to see much that's out of
that zone, however. New Yorkers in particular are always stunned when
by some odd chance they look up and notice what's on the second and
third floors of the buildings they pass every day. There's an entire level
of business windows in crowded midtown Manhattan that are like an
open secret. The job of seducing people up or down a flight of stairs is
not an American strength. In New York, there is a long tradition of mar-
ginal businesses trying to cling to the upper and sometimes lower registers of our vision. Those attempts usually contain some kind of display,
or signage at the very least. However, they're hidden in plain sight.

But when visitors come to town, they walk and look according to
rules and habits acquired elsewhere—like at the mall. In cities they do
that little gee-whiz-ma-lookit-how-tall-*that*-one-is dance when seeing
a real skyscraper up close. Native walkers will sometimes come upon a
group of people standing stock-still, looking at some fixed point high on
a building's facade, and be briefly misled into thinking there's something of genuine interest up there—like a jumper, or maybe King
Kong. Then we look a little closer and realize we've been fooled by a
bunch of bedazzled tourists, or an effete architectural walking tour. Do
we care about what the Municipal Art Society thinks is significant on
that facade? That's when we sneer and shoulder our way past, irritated
at being had by a bunch of rubes.

There's something so innocent, so childlike and trusting, about how tourists walk in a city. They lack pedestrian radar, that combination of peripheral vision, hard-won experience, and ESP that alerts you to the taxi that's about to occupy the space where you're standing, or the bike messenger who's speeding into your intended path. Neither do visiting walkers anticipate the usual urban decision points. For instance, veteran city walkers will usually begin to plot a turn well before they reach the corner, whereas visiting pedestrians stroll as though they'll be continuing in that direction indefinitely; when they do hit an intersection they halt, convene, swivel in all directions, and only *then* begin to figure out where they'll go and by what path they'll go there. Urbanites use a special body vocabulary, from a dropped shoulder to a shifted briefcase, that tells fellow travelers our intentions.

In the city, and especially in the hectic districts where stores and shopping predominate, people move with a great sense of purpose. No matter where you're headed, you tend to go as though you're on some mission of high importance. Partly it's because no self-respecting urban dweller wants to admit, even by the implication of a leisurely gait, that he or she is not urgently needed somewhere else. But it's also the way that we internalize the rhythms and the velocity of the city. The late William H. Whyte, the distinguished American Urbanist and my friend, used to say that the pace and character of New Yorkers was set by the traffic lights. They trained us to walk as fast as possible, so that we can make it through the next intersection without stopping for a red light. He discovered that the stoplight cycles form us into what he called pedestrian platoons—a crowd builds at a crosswalk, waiting for the green light, at which point we all hurry forward in a cluster until we are stopped by the next red light. If you're watching from above, you see that while the groups spread out slightly as they move forward, the pattern is densely packed sidewalk followed by long, mostly empty stretches. Twenty years ago, Lexington Avenue at lunchtime was the most crowded stretch of pavement in Manhattan, with some four thousand people moving in an hour through a twelve-and-a-half-foot space. I'd argue that in 2003, sections of Canal Street on Saturday rival the density of Hong Kong and Shanghai, or the entrance to the Spice Market in Istanbul.

I spent hours at Tokyo's Shibuya Station watching the train and subway stations push out shoppers as if from a fire hose, spraying them across a broad square and into a fan of arterial streets. The plaza outside the station is a dense staging area combining all the classic elements of great urban public space—a little shade, places to lean or sit, formal and informal selling from stores and kiosks, and music. There is enough of a cross section of humanity to make everyone feel comfortable, while at the same time providing everyone with someone to gawk at. The sea of hairstyles and costumes makes New York's East Village look tame. It is a great show.

Like many commercial districts in Japan, the electronic signage is overwhelming. Beyond the huge screens playing rock videos, electronic advertising is shotgunned across every facade. Appearing on those video screens in Shibuya Square is the dream of every aspiring Japanese rapper. Doe-eyed high school girls cluster in pods, staring at the screens, thumbs flying across the keypads on their oversize cell phones as they punch out instant messages. At seemingly regular intervals sound trucks blaring political messages roll through the square, their distorted voices careening across the high-rise windows and plate-glass department store facades. The background noise is constant; music, taxis, announcements from the station all carried on the smell of salty food and burnt diesel.

The square's main intersection is a series of five converging streets. At the crosswalks, the crowd surges ten to twelve people deep. The patience of the Tokyo pedestrian is rooted alternatively in Zen and fast food. Cars pull slowly through the intersection, and people are careful not to look at one another, but the mounting sense of impatient energy is palpable. As the light changes, the octagonal street transforms into a surreal barn dance as thousands of people charge around oblique corners in ordered chaos. The pace of the dance is a steady, manic cadence—however driven or desperate you might be, you can't move any faster. Bodies pass close enough to give secondhand hits of tobacco and the faux-fruit fragrance of the month. Especially in summer, the ripples of body heat are a triumph of human radar and coordination as everyone brushes but no one touches. They watch their feet and feel their polite insignificance because in a shopping district all pedestrians carry the same residual weight.

Shibuya is one of the world's busiest commercial corners; the shopping extends two levels below the street in some places and six to ten levels above. The entire coming and going is funneled through sidewalks only three to four yards wide. The compression is palpable, which is part of the attraction, while at the same time exhausting. It is a mosh pit that predates punk.

The experience of a city, whether New York or Tokyo, is in great contrast to how walking is performed in malls. There, for starters, the surface is reliability itself—usually some smooth petrochemical product, either linoleum or vinyl or acrylic. In the swankier districts, such as the one we're in today, you may find tiles made of ceramic or stone, but these are no less dedicated to the safety and comfort of the walker. There will be no obstacles or surprises of any kind down there on the floor itself—the rules of the mall guarantee this much, and the store leases, the legal contracts that define the environment, require it. As a result, looking down while walking in a mall is utterly pointless. There's nothing down there to see. This is a matter of trust. Only the most crabbed and paranoid pedestrian looks at the floor in a mall.

Similarly, in a mall you walk safe in the knowledge that everyone is there to do the exact same thing you're doing, however we define the complex set of missions you've undertaken. There are no bicycle messengers, careening taxis, distracted truck drivers, no hell-bent young career women storming past, shouldering you out of the way, no office drones racing through a lunch hour's worth of errands, no mobs of high school kids out frolicking, pretending they own the sidewalk. Nobody here but us shoppers. The corridors are unipurpose. We are all in agreement about why we are here. With that homogeneity of intention comes safety.

Safety is also defined here by the lack of any of the menaces we routinely face when we're out in the wild. As we've said, there's no crime here, at least none where anyone can see it. No bad weather, either, no wind, no rain. No spitters, even, or cigarette-butt flickers. No litterbugs. No dogs. Life under that big mall roof is safe and warm and slow. (Doesn't sound so bad that way, does it?) And the walking pace in here is a reflection of the wider lassitude. Interestingly, on a city street men walk faster than women; in a mall the positions are reversed, since men tend to wander malls like semi-lost children, whereas women are the ones who inhabit the place with a true shopper's sense of purpose.

There's even a term for it—poky pedestrians are known as *meanderthals*. But the use of *mall walker* as a term of derision has been around for some time. That refers to the speed but also to the practice of strolling three, four, or more abreast. In the city, "if we try and go three across, it slows us down," confessed a mall walker from Birmingham, Alabama, to a *New York Times* reporter writing about the tense life of a Manhattan pedestrian. Most people drive a lot and walk little, so they forget how it's done. Will future generations have to take walker's ed in high school?

In a city store, speed overall is much more important to shoppers than it is in a mall. A company we've studied routinely deploys twice as many cashiers at its store near Wall Street than it does in a branch of roughly the same size located in a mall. Mall shoppers are willing to wait a little longer. City shoppers are not. City shoppers have bigger fish to fry, while mall shoppers don't—even when they're the exact same people. The mall makes them more patient. Conversion rate is higher in a mall, too—in a city store, shoppers race in, look around for what they need, become frustrated when they can't find it immediately, and split. In a mall, you'll take a little longer, consult a sales associate, and in the end find what you're looking for.

❖   ❖   ❖

In cities we have systems that help us figure out where we are. Fixed landmarks (tall buildings, subway entrances) combined with dynamic references (streets, sun position, shadow lines) keep us oriented. It's also socially acceptable to ask for directions in a city. Being lost is stressful, and the stress is exacerbated in a mall. Because it is a planned environment, there is no such thing as being deliciously lost in the mall.

In malls, way-finding requires maps, and when malls meet cartography, the result is not magic. To be fair, cartography often relies on some generally understood basic reference points: North is *that way*, or Fifth Avenue is *over there*. Having stepped from the featureless parking lot through a mouse-hole entrance, is there any surprise that we are disoriented? Some malls attempt to name interior corridors as though they were streets, but such efforts generally fail. At best, the quadrants of the mall are recognized by the anchors—oh, that's the Sears side, or the Bloomingdale's end.

Stopping to ask for directions in a mall is often an exercise in frustration. There is no tradition of talking to, much less helping, strangers in a mall. This is not to say that people aren't friendly—they just seem surprised that someone is talking to them. Some people know only one small section of a mall. Even some sales associates know only their immediate surroundings. Security guards are surprised even to be noticed, much less stopped and solicited for help.

A map at the entrance seems like a good idea, until you actually come across one. Do all mall maps stink? In our studies of people in shopping centers, we've timed how long they spend staring at those big, lighted board mall directories. In one study the average was twenty-two seconds. That's a *very* long time to study a map. Too long. It indicates that a fair number of people never find what they're looking for—shoppers struggle to decipher the map and then just give up. They walk away in frustration. Malls are too huge and, unlike when driving, you move at will throughout a mall. And it may exist on two or three levels, adding to the complexity. The directories in most malls look like they were designed for electricians—like wiring guides. They don't look like malls. Shoppers negotiate spaces better if they have fixed points to guide them, like "Shoes over here" or "Escalator there."

Department stores might also benefit by placing maps instead of directories right inside the doorway. Without them, you stand in the entrance and look out over the floor of the store with absolutely no idea of what you're looking at. It's just a huge expanse of undifferentiated space. There's a sea of merchandise.

Here's what a good store map would look like. It would be horizontal, like a tabletop, instead of vertical like most mall maps. You could look down on it, at waist-level, find what you need—say, the shoe department, and then look up to locate it for real. You can't do that standing behind an eight-foot-tall board.

My perfect store map would use symbols. If, for example, the ladies' shoe department was on the left-hand side of this floor, halfway back, there would be a big shoe on the left side of the map, halfway back. Maybe I'd even have a huge shoe hanging from the ceiling over the shoe department, so you could see it from the entrance.

Maps in department stores and malls are important because, when properly designed, they can help avert shopper frustration. You could argue that a shopper who is temporarily lost may wander deeper into a store and discover sections she or he might otherwise have missed. But it's more likely that the shopper will grow exasperated and impatient, leading to walkouts, lost sales, and ill will.

In the course of our research we watch thousands upon thousands of people shop every year. In some instances, they spend time in a store because they're enjoying it, or they're accomplishing things. That's good. But in other cases, they're spending time in the store because it's so badly designed and stocked that it takes forever to find things. That's not good. We draw the paths that people follow—we call them "tracks"—on paper maps of a store's floor plan. You should see the track for a lost shopper—it goes a little ways in this direction, stops, goes off over there, stops again, retraces itself back to the starting point, then goes off on a totally different path. You can look at it and feel the shopper seething. Before long, the track goes right back out the door.

Men dart in, look around, refuse to ask for help, try two or three directions, give up, and split. Boom. All a store can do is accommodate male nature by putting the goods men buy near the entrances and making the signs big and clear.

Not long ago I toured a mall with a female executive I know. We had never been there before and tried to make use of the mall map, which was the typical vertical affair.

"Where's the little YOU ARE HERE symbol?" she asked. "Even that's tough to find."

"That's true," said an elderly man trying to study the map over our shoulders.

"Is this helpful?" I asked.

"I've only been here one time before. I don't live around here, my daughter does. And the first time I tried using this map it took me two minutes just to find the YOU ARE HERE thingy. And look at it—it's just a little sticker somebody stuck on here. It even covers a whole store!"

An entire business wiped out by an instrument meant to help shoppers to find stores.

"The other day I saw an interesting mall map—it was a Coke machine with the map on its side," my friend said.

"How was the map?"

"Same as this. Same as all the rest."

"But you could buy a Coke from it?"

"Yeah. Considering how long people end up staring at these maps, it was a pretty awesome product placement. What would improve these maps, really?"

"Voice-recognition software maybe. You could ask the map, 'Where's the Banana Republic for women?' and a trail of tiny lightbulbs on the map would guide you from where you're standing to where the store is located. Or even better, they could install tiny lightbulbs in the actual floor of the mall, and when you ask for a store the floor itself would light up. You could just follow the bulbs to your destination."

"That's not a map, that's a guide."

In theory, there *is* something meant to perform that function: the mall's customer service desk. Every mall has one of these. They're intended to fulfill a narrow range of tasks: pointing lost shoppers in the right direction; selling mall gift certificates, reuniting lost kiddies with their keepers, and so on. Some malls use these desks to gather names for mailing lists—they give you a bogus gift or mall membership card, and in exchange they get your name on their database, free of charge. It's a lot cheaper than buying mailing lists from direct marketers.

These desks might clear up a certain amount of shopper confusion, except that many malls defeat the purpose by placing them in a less-than-prominent location. Often, you need assistance just to find the assistance desk.

The key to a sense of place is often a human face. Management in malls is passive as far as the customer is concerned. While the premise of the mall is that we customers should wander, and that the longer they hold us the more we'll spend, many of us are making our shopping choices based on an understanding of how the layout works. For both male-hunter and female-gatherer, whether at the mall or in the woods, our use of shortcuts demonstrates our expertise. Teaching us to use the right mouse hole is also ensuring that we return. No expert shopper looks at a map, or visits the customer service desk, unless they must.

7 Nose and Toes

AT LAST, a store. The shopping begins.

You might think that retailers would fight to be nearest the entrances. But take a look at what's here, just inside the doorway. A hair salon on one side and a store that sells exercise equipment on the other. The beauty parlor is nearly full, although you can bet these are regular customers, not mall shoppers who have decided on impulse to get a cut and color. The exercise store is empty, which makes sense—how many treadmills does the average consumer buy? If the shop sells one or two it's a good day. You'll sometimes find banks in these locations, another low-profile tenant. Post offices. Video game arcades. Why is it that the least attractive tenants get these high-traffic positions?

Call it the mall's decompression zone. The fact is that when we enter any building, we need a series of steps just to make the adjustment between out there and in here. You need to slow your walk a little, allow your eyes to adjust to the change in lighting, give your senses a chance to detect changes in temperature and so on. You walk through any door and suddenly your brain has to take in a load of new information and process it so you'll feel oriented. You're not really ready to make any buying decisions for the first ten or fifteen feet. This transition stage is one of the most critical things we've learned in two decades of studying how shoppers move through retail environments. Nothing too close to the door really registers. If there's a sign, you probably won't read it. If there's a display of merchandise, you'll barely notice it. Some stores have the bad habit of stacking shopping baskets just inside the doorway. People zoom right past them.

Because of this transition zone, the best stores in the mall are never near the entrance. The reasoning is simple—the mall owner charges every tenant a flat rent based on space plus a percentage of sales. So it's in the mall's own interest to have the hottest stores in the prime locations, inside. Because this particular doorway feels like a secondary entrance, only a small portion of all shoppers will even see these shops. Fewer eyeballs equals fewer bucks. That equation is the basis for all mall math. And that's why underachievers go nearest the door. When entering a mall, your eye is immediately drawn way up ahead, to the heart of the place. That's where you want to be. So let's join everybody else speeding past the ladies under the hair dryers. We've got a date.

⁂ ⁂ ⁂

My friend Carol understands a thing or two about shopping and malls. She's a fortyish woman who has spent plenty of her own time in stores. But she's also an executive with a major corporation that specializes in selling things to women shoppers. Carol's expertise is visual merchandising, meaning she's responsible for everything her company puts on the floor of a store—the product, the displays, the signs, the whole thing, from sea to shining sea. So she knows her stuff.

She's also fun to shop with.

Carol had requested that we rendezvous near a little-used doorway in one of the mall's department stores. It's a smart move for at least one reason—the parking lot right outside here is never crowded.

"This is the entrance for somebody who really *knows* the mall," says Carol as she breezes through the door.

"Good call," I say.

This entrance takes us into Filene's, the famous Boston-based retailer, but not to the heart of the store. It takes us right into men's underwear.

Men's underwear is the bottom of the barrel where Filene's is concerned, no doubt about it. This stuff sells twice a year, when it goes on sale. No man has ever come here to buy underwear. Their wives and girlfriends shop for them. Otherwise, it's the dead zone.

"Being a single woman, I don't need to pay *any* attention to men's stuff," Carol says. "But this door gets me right to cosmetics. And there's something else that makes this a great entrance."

"Which is?"

"The bathrooms are right over there."

"And the elevators and escalators."

"It's interesting," Carol says, "how this out-of-the-way entrance puts us right into cosmetics and ladies' shoes, two of the most heavily trafficked areas of the store. People in the company probably thought it was crazy to put shoes and cosmetics across the aisle from each other because they couldn't see the connection. All they saw was why take two successful departments and put them close together? Where, in reality, being together like this makes each department even stronger."

"Because?"

"Because think about it: You're standing in the shoe department, you've told the salesperson which styles you want to see in your size, and now you're waiting for her to get back. You're not going to keep looking at shoes, because you've already done that—you did it *before* you sent the clerk away to get your size. Most logical thing in the world. So now where do you look? You look across the aisle at the cosmetics counters. You see all these things you want to try. And especially if you don't find anything to buy in the shoe department. You can walk right across the aisle and find something there."

"How did the executives miss that connection?"

"Because the connection is all in the heads of the women shoppers, and it was probably men making the decisions about what would go where. What do shoes and lipstick have in common? Nothing. But because men don't shop for shoes like women do, they don't know what it's like to be a woman standing around for five minutes waiting for your size to arrive."

"Wait a sec—sure they do."

"Well, then maybe men just don't behave like women do. Women want to look at something while they wait. They want to *shop*. I bet some woman had to point out to the store-planning executives that placing shoes and cosmetics close together was a good idea."

This is the kind of thing that comes up every day in my line of work watching people in stores. Any time a shopper is standing or sitting around with nothing to do, the retailer has got something to deal with. Problem or opportunity? It can go either way. Boredom makes time crawl. Interest makes it race. If a woman is bored waiting for the clerk to return with her shoes, the wait feels longer than it really is. The problem becomes an opportunity when, in instances such as this one, the retailer fills the empty moments in a potentially productive fashion. If there were something for that shopper to browse—some other category of goods, like bags, or even something totally unrelated—I don't know, laptop computers—it could work. "While you're waiting for your shoes, take a look at the slim new Apple notebooks we just got in. . . ."

If jamming the shoe department with unrelated merchandise feels like a bad idea, the retailer could try a message of some kind or other. Maybe a video catalog of what's new in the sportswear department. Maybe a sign explaining the store's made-to-measure suits. A good, long sign with lots of words would be sensible here—you've got a captive audience for at least two minutes, and they'd be grateful for something absorbing.

Or, as Filene's has done, you could put cosmetics adjacent to shoes. It's a smart move—the makeup counters and shelves are big and graphic enough to see from this distance. Makeovers are also an activity and one of the reasons we go to the mall to get some action. Smart cosmetics companies vie to be near shoe departments in stores such as this. Of course, only one side of the cosmetics section can be facing the shoe department. So *really* smart cosmetics companies insist on being on the side that faces the shoes instead of, say, the side facing the handbag department. Smart stores have learned to treat anything that faces ladies' shoes as prime real estate.

"But there *is* a potential downside to this," I point out.

"Which is?"

"Shallow loop."

"Oh, right."

Let's say there's a woman out there who needs shoes and cosmetics. Two staples of malls and of women's lives. A smart shopper, one who really knows this mall, can park in our little-used lot, run in, get the shoes, get the cosmetics, and run back out to continue her busy day. That's a good thing, right? Maybe that woman would get her shoes and cosmetics elsewhere if she didn't know how easy Filene's makes it for her. The juxtaposition of these two departments here creates a third department—the shoe/mascara section—and drives sales.

But I could just as easily argue that putting two strong departments together like this squanders the power of each, individually, to attract shoppers. Carol alluded to that—why put two magnets side by side when you can separate them and have each one draw women to their respective parts of the store? It's an old dilemma in retailing. Supermarket layouts always used to put the dairy case in the rearmost corner of the store, on the theory that everybody had to buy milk, meaning they'd all traipse through the rest of the store to get it. A sound practice, except that it gave rise to the convenience store as the supermarket's prime competitor. Instead of making it hard to buy milk, the C-store made it easy—you park, run inside, grab the milk (which was probably within thirty feet of the door), pay, and are on your way. In response, some supermarkets created little C-stores within the store, just inside the entrance. If all you really needed was milk, you could get it and go. That's the shallow loop—instead of going from the front door to the rear and back to the front again, you barely penetrate the store.

Which layout makes more sense? Each approach sacrifices something. The old-fashioned strategy for luring shoppers through the store works. But it makes getting what you want and getting out a little less convenient. Once shoppers caught on, they began to feel manipulated. Which is not a good thing.

"If you know this mall well, you know you can get in and out in twenty minutes. Today, speed is everything for most women," Carol says. "This is good for the shopper."

"Though it could be bad for the retailer," I add.

"Well, I guess the retailer is going to have to figure something out."

                              ❁   ❁   ❁

Shopping with Carol is always productive for me because we tend to focus on what the process is like for women, and women are the primary actors in the world of shopping. Especially mall shopping.

The big theory of stores once held that women liked spending time in them because it was their main method of interacting with the world of grown-ups—of business and finance and money. They were home all day with the kids, and then home all night, too. Their husbands were completely exhausted by their involvement in the world of commerce, and seeking a little bit of respite from it. Whereas she hungered for a life of adult concerns and activities.

The midcentury shift to the suburbs only increased female isolation. Now there was no such thing as a stroll down the street to the cleaners or the appliance store or the dress shop, since no place could be easily reached by walking, and in suburbia, even if you did walk, you didn't enjoy any of the happenstance meetings a city stroll afforded. Step outside your city door, and there was the world, filled with activity and purpose and hustle. Step outside your suburban door and there was . . . another homemaker, stepping outside her door, looking back at you.

You can see how shopping at the mall came to seem like an appealing activity. It wasn't everything a woman could wish for, true, but it was quite a bit better than anything else available.

The mall rose up in response to the suburban existence, but it actually came along on the cusp of yet another major demographic shift, one that would throw shopping centers for a loop. By the 1980s, a great many of those suburban homemakers had begun working outside the home, either full- or part-time. Roughly two-thirds of adult American women today work outside the home. Their infusion into the world of work is what made the past two decades of middle-class life so materially splendid, even extravagant. And it left women with a lot less time for the mall. Their lives became crunched, and the world of retailing—stores, restaurants, and banking—had to respond. Women became the most avid users of ATMs, for instance, contrary to what the banking gurus expected. Women weren't scared off by the new technology; in fact, in the workplace, they were the ones required to master innovations in hardware and software. Women were also caught most severely between competing responsibilities at work and at home (and in the commute between the two, which, again, affected suburban women most direly).

The restaurant and retail food industries have been utterly transformed by the needs of women who work. "Meal replacement" has become the hottest growth area in the food industry. Supermarkets are forever increasing the space devoted to making and selling of prepared foods—you can't find a market today that doesn't include a bakery, charcuterie, soup station, salad bar, sushi chef. And what the supermarket doesn't do, the fast-food and family-restaurant chains do. We can complain all we like about the quality and nutritional value of the food these businesses provide—and we might start by wondering if there's any connection between the boom in prepared meals and the obesity epidemic—but we must give them their due when it comes to identifying and meeting a need.

How have the malls done in that regard? If women are at work, they're not at the shopping center. The very nature of the relationship between the woman shopper and the mall has been jeopardized. She no longer has the time to spend hours there, moving from shop to shop at a leisurely pace. She may now have to run in, grab what's necessary, then run out. Unless, of course, the mall can respond to the changes in her life with changes of its own.

Which brings us around to cosmetics. The beauty business is hardball, and yet it's full of voodoo, just as you might expect. It represents the triumph of hope over greed. There are many labels, each with its own niche and devotees, but for the most part the firms all buy their products from the same small group of factories. The cost of a lipstick and its packaging is around a dollar or so. The rest is marketing, distribution, and a whole lot of profit.

The world of beauty used to be divided into two classes—the stuff sold at mass-market retailers (drugstores, supermarkets, discounters) and what went to the fancy cosmetics salons in department stores. Think Revlon, Cover Girl, and Maybelline at the former, versus Lancôme and Estée Lauder at the latter. It was a tidy little world, until competition came along and opened up some exciting new channels. Suddenly there were boutique brands sold directly through their own stores, such as Bobbi Brown, MAC, and Aveda. The French retailer Sephora came along with its sophisticated European stores and suddenly the world of beauty retailing became a lot less orderly and a lot more interesting, at least for the customers.

Let's look at just one product—hair color. When she's sixteen, hair color is a girl's fashion accessory. My goddaughter spent her teenage years changing the color of her hair every ten minutes. It was fun and easy. By twenty-three she had made peace with the color God gave her, which didn't stop her from coloring it for special events or to annoy her mother. It was still a fashion statement.

For most women, hair color starts to get serious at around age thirty-five. The search for her proper hue gets narrower, and the range of experimentation becomes focused and purposeful. By her mid-forties, hair coloring is a staple. She renews the coloring on a fixed schedule, whether at the salon or at home.

Cosmetics moves in the same arc, from play to necessity. For the young customer it is dress up. It's entertainment, and the range of options is governed by price and brand appeal. Most middle-class, middle-aged American women started buying cosmetics at the drugstore. Gen-X and Gen-Y got their start at Kmart, Target, or Wal-Mart, or at the supermarket, as the distribution of cosmetics fanned out. Historically, the department store sold to well-off middle-aged women. The price difference between a drugstore lipstick at $6 and the fancy department store brand at $22 is a big jump, even though the difference in quality is slight.

Like hair color, makeup started out as fun and became a serious aspect of a woman's presentation to the world. As it traversed that span, it moved from the drugstore to the department store and went up in price. The ritual of putting on one's face in the morning and using restorative products at night was set.

The difference between mass and class (the industry term for the drugstore/Kmart/Wal-Mart and Filene's/Bloomingdale's/Burdines) was well defined until about ten years ago, when the lines started to blur. Today, the orderly world of cosmetics is gone. Some women shop both ends. They buy Revlon nail polish at the drugstore and Clinique face products at the department store. Women whose economic situations improved no longer reliably traded up from L'Oréal to Lancôme. Those women didn't like the way goods were being sold to them; they especially resented the peculiar industry practice of not putting price tags on the goods. Many women were too intimidated to demand to know what they were spending, and walked away from the department store counter having shelled out a lot more than they were expecting to pay.

Sephora opened up a new world by introducing "open sell." Traditionally, the salesperson at the department store was necessary to the transaction—she was the go-between linking you the shopper to the cosmetics manufacturer. Letting women examine and try the products changed the nature of the relationship. It put the customer in charge and turned the sales associate into her makeup pal.

Department stores' hold on the high-end cosmetics market has weakened, but makeup counters still occupy the prime real estate at the front of the store. That's due to the universal appeal of makeup, but equally to the fact that it is a high-margin category.

"They're willing to make less profit on apparel," Carol explains, "so long as they can make more on mascara. A mascara dollar is worth more than a dress dollar."

We stop walking a second and look around at the spectacle before us. There's something Felliniesque about a department store cosmetics section. You stand here on a Saturday morning, dressed in the standard mall-casual suburban wardrobe, gazing at a chamber glittering with chandeliers, populated by saleswomen wearing makeup and hair dramatic enough for opening night at La Scala. Their faces are like masks of pale, poreless skin, ruby-red lips, smoldering eye treatments—positively kabuki-like. They're almost intimidating.

The purchase of cosmetics is as public as a private art form gets. It isn't quite a massage, but it is an intimate act between two consenting adults. The beauty adviser will perform a makeover and offer advice, at the end of which you may simply walk away without making a purchase. So a good beauty adviser needs to build a following among her customers. Some cosmetic lines, such as Trish McEvoy, drive their business by staging mass makeover events where teams of "expert stylists," including Trish herself, run marathon sessions. It's quite a show—it sells a lot of cosmetics and builds a devoted following.

I've always been fascinated by how selling cosmetics resembles fishing. The sales associate needs to get involved, but she can't rush things. If she offers help too soon, the shopper can easily demur and walk away. In fact, we learned that if the clerk approaches the shopper within the first thirty seconds, it scares her away. The trick is to let the customer browse unaided, then watch her carefully for the first time she raises her head, even for a second. That means she's found something she might want but needs a little information. It's the equivalent of a jerk on a fishing line—that's the moment the sales associate needs to start reeling her in.

Cosmetics seem to be everywhere in this mall. In addition to department stores, you also have at least three or four cosmetics boutiques—the specialty shops like MAC and Sephora and so on. And some of the stores that sell women's clothing also sell cosmetics. Victoria's Secret now does an entire companion store for cosmetics and bath and so on. And there's a drugstore, if not actually in the mall then very close by.

Women will shop for cosmetics just about anywhere. If a store can get a woman to look into a mirror, it can sell her lipstick or blusher. One hot new line of cosmetics is sold only through plastic surgeons' offices. The thing that male researchers misunderstand is *how* most women buy cosmetics. Overwhelmingly, they purchase cosmetics on impulse—a woman approaches the counter, looks into the mirror, realizes that her lips could stand some color. So she begins to shop to meet that immediate need. She may also buy because she's low on mascara or she lost her favorite eyebrow pencil. But by and large it's for right now.

Here's another bit of voodoo in the world of high-end cosmetics. They never go on sale. *Ever.* Because women, it is thought, will not buy discounted cosmetics. It feels wrong. They'll buy anything else marked down as low as possible. The other day I came upon a huddle of sophisticated young Manhattan women, shivering outside on the coldest day of the year, waiting in line at the Manolo Blahnik sale. Women will risk hypothermia to save money on stiletto heels, but cut-rate cosmetics feels like you're putting something ratty on your face.

So instead of sales, the manufacturers offer something known as gift-with-purchase. Spend this much today, and you get this free gift package containing blah, blah, blah—a $25 value. The point is to give you the sensation of having saved $25 without having to discount the cosmetics. That system has been in place for probably thirty years now. The gift is intended to introduce eager shoppers to new products. But the industry has found that if there are three free things, maybe the customer will use two and come back to buy one. Cosmetics executives rue the day the gift-with-purchase policy began, but it's now a habit neither they nor their customers can break.

"There's a final issue playing out in cosmetics," I say.

"Which is?"

"The level of importance of anything women put on either nose or toes."

For most women, those are the areas that matter most. The extremes—the face and hair and the feet. When choosing a jacket or a skirt, there's some leeway for color and style and fit. Even in underwear. Most women are not expecting absolute perfection. But when you're talking about makeup or shoes, the standards suddenly go way up. No woman is going to settle.

"And women *always* shop those two departments, don't they?" I ask.

"Yes," says Carol, "it's something I notice when I shop with my sister or my friends. No matter what else we look at, we always go through cosmetics and shoes. You just do. If we're shopping a high-end store or a discounter, no difference. It's like you can't *not* go. Even if it means you're just sort of walking through and browsing because you're looking for something that gets you excited."

"I want you to give me a little guided tour of the counters here."

"Okay. Well, the first thing you may have noticed here is that there's almost no real selling space. Look at this counter."

It's a typical cosmetics counter.

"On the counter you have your visual here—the sign that announces they're giving away a free gift. Next to that is your tester unit, with a small sign giving some price information. But where do you do your selling? Where's a little bit of empty counter where you and the shopper can talk and put a few possible purchases down?

"Come over into this area—you've got a major tester unit showing all the different shades of lipstick, then you've got a smaller color thing, and now we finally find maybe six inches of horizontal space. And a mirror, too, at last. So it's four or five feet of solid merchandise without a single mirror. I don't care where you go or which cosmetics counter you visit, nobody understands the mirror, which should be the simplest thing here. It's what cosmetics counters should be built around. How can you buy cosmetics without a mirror?"

This is a major problem in the cosmetics department. Insufficient mirrors. Not only too few, but also too small, and not well positioned, and not properly illuminated. This is true despite the fact that the mirror is the one thing that every woman shopping here really *wants* to see. She wants to see what's in the mirror. That's what she's buying. Not the poster. Not the lighting. If cosmetics departments were designed for the way women really use them, there would be plenty of mirrors, all at the right height. A shopper would be able to see her face from twenty paces away. It's what would draw her in. And all the expensive, flattering lighting would be trained on the shoppers' faces, not on Elizabeth Hurley's.

However, you can quickly scan the department and figure out which furnishings were thought to be most critical by the retailer. The graphics—the big, expensive posters, replicas of the big, expensive ads that ran in *Vanity Fair* and *Vogue*—are beautifully realized and prominently displayed and advantageously illuminated by spotlights. Somebody believes in these ads. The merchandise comes second.

You might think that given enough time and money, somebody would solve the problem of cosmetic tester units. But it hasn't happened yet. The challenge is to come up with a display that shows all the various shades of lipstick or powder or eye shadow and so forth, and allows the woman to try a few herself. This hunk of plastic (which is what it usually is) is the keystone of the open-sell method of cosmetics retailing. Without it—without giving women a way to see what that shade looks like on her skin—it all comes to naught. Women are always looking for something new in cosmetics. Even if they love the shade of lipstick they're using now, they're keen to find something newer, or better.

Each of these testers starts life looking attractive and inviting, brimming with shades and textures and so on. Then it hits the store, and all hell breaks loose. Women start using them! And that's where the illusion begins to disintegrate. In order to touch one pot of lip gloss, it is almost impossible to avoid dragging your cuff through three others. Or as soon as you pick up one pencil, all the rest go rolling onto the floor.

"They're struggling with pencils, too," Carol says. "*Everybody* has a problem with pencils. Nobody has figured out how to sell the pencil piece in an open-sell environment. And the lipstick presentation leaves a lot to be desired. The cleanliness problem is *the* number-one issue. Cleanliness is critical. Your lips are a very personal area."

"Don't you think the mirrors should be magnified?" I ask. "You know, as we get older, our eyes get worse. And the older shoppers are the ones who really need makeup, more than the kids do."

"Absolutely. But the companies don't design these departments to make the shopper the star. To them, the star of this counter is the supermodel or the celebrity who's in the ad campaign. After all, they paid her a ton of money—she *must* be the star. After her, the secondary star is the lady who is selling the product. Then, in last place, comes the customer. It's totally wrong."

"And the lights here are *horrible.* . . ."

That wasn't Carol or me—it was the sales associate, a very pleasant-seeming lady who has been quietly eavesdropping but now has her own two cents to contribute.

"They really are, aren't they?" Carol sympathizes. "Fluorescent lights give everything a yellow cast. It makes it hard to know what a color really will look like."

"Well, that's why I suggest that they go over to that full-length mirror there, near the window."

"You see?" Carol says. "That's what a good salesperson does. How long have you been here?"

"Two years in November. Are you people with the main office?" the saleslady asks us. "Because if you are, we have no product here on the floor."

"Yeah, I can see that," Carol says.

"The shelves are empty. I have nothing to offer. I am absolutely down on everything. And I won't sell my customers something that's wrong for them."

"That's great."

"Because then she'll never come back to me. I don't make customers, I make friends."

"As it should be," Carol says.

"Well, have a lovely day. It's a shame you have to spend it in here like I do."

"Oh, no," Carol says. "We're shopping. This is fun."

8 *Sex and the Mall*

NOW WE'RE leaving cosmetics behind and strolling the rest of the mall. We've gone a few paces before we come upon a window display that stops us, which is what they're supposed to do.

We're looking into the window of H&M, the giant Swedish apparel chain. They've done an outstanding job of cornering the market for what I call disposable clothes—garments that look really trendy and stylish but cost around $25 or less. Teenagers worship H&M. The window is populated by sylphlike mannequins, reed-thin representations of your average postadolescent girl-woman. Not one of them is dressed in anything you'd expect to see worn at Sunday school.

"My niece will *make* my sister take her to H&M every time they visit me in New York," Carol says. "My sister likes the prices but hates the styles."

"Some of it's like hooker wear, isn't it?"

"Teenage hooker wear."

"Older people look at how girls dress, with the belly exposed and hipbones exposed and the tight, flimsy tops and skin-tight pants, and it alarms them. But young girls have no idea what a hooker looks like or even what a hooker *is*. To her, it's just how glamorous young women look today."

"The other thing to keep in mind is that grandmothers today also dress less conservatively than ever before. When the line moves, it moves for everybody."

We move a few stores along, until the window with the number-one "capture rate" in any mall in America stops us again.

"Here's where mall sex really started," Carol says.

"Is that what Victoria's Secret is selling?"

"I think it's selling sex *appeal*. Inexpensive sex appeal. Women visit this store to get in touch with their feminine side. The company has taken underwear from being a staple to being something where there's a personal connection. This is especially true for women thirty-five and younger. Though I always wonder what the woman who's over thirty-five is supposed to do about getting in touch with *her* feminine side.

"Another example of how the mall reflects real life—because when women hit a certain age, society stops thinking of them as sexy. The stores are an example of that. Compare the H&M window with a window aimed at the fifty-year-old woman."

"Susan Sarandon must be pushing fifty-five."

"Sophia Loren passed sixty many moons ago. Where do you think she shops?"

"The funny part is that while Victoria's Secret sells modestly priced goods, older women could and absolutely *would* pay a good deal more for lingerie," I point out. "They're the ones who have the higher disposable income, and their tastes are more sophisticated. They're ready to splurge a little on themselves, to go along with the pedicures, facials, body waxings, spa treatments, and botox. They'd pay big bucks for gorgeous, high-quality underwear. If only somebody would sell it to them."

"There *are* fancier brands of lingerie, but sold either in department stores or in boutiques. Victoria's Secret has a special label for older shoppers, but I think the company is missing a bet by not opening a separate chain of stores for them. They could call it Victoria's Mother's Secret."

"They're also not aggressively serving the plus-size woman of *any* age," I say. "Now, maybe they don't want older or bigger women because they're afraid it would drive away the young, thin shopper. But it seems there must be a way for them to go after those other markets, too."

"Especially when you consider that a substantial percentage of the population of American women is overweight," says Carol. "And they're not even all old. I see a lot of fat teenagers and women in their twenties."

"Well, there *is* a high fashion chain now for young chubbies."

"I've seen it. There's a chain of stores called Torrid. And the clothes they sell are *sexy*."

"Yes indeed. Big young girls tend to get big in the right places."

"And they're not bashful, either. As long as they're fat and curvy, they can make it work. Major cleavage. Narrow at the waist and tight on the butt."

"This is one of those weird gulfs between media imagery and real life," I say. "Judging by the fashion magazines you'd think that women would be ashamed to be overweight. Judging by how the weight of the average American girl has gone up, though, you get the opposite impression. But even if Victoria's Secret carried big sizes, could big girls get away with wearing this stuff?"

"Like thongs, you mean?"

"Well, yeah."

"Big girls wear thongs, believe me," Carol says. "And they buy them here, too. You won't see plus-size mannequins, but thong sizes absolutely go up to extra-large, you'll notice."

"Victoria's Secret really *did* make it okay for the average young woman to wear racy underwear."

"Yes," says Carol, "and the advantage of the low prices is that you can wear the stuff as long as it's fun, then replace it. This is where girls go when they first begin buying their own underwear. This is how they announce, 'My mom doesn't buy my underwear anymore.' Victoria's Secret sells hottie underwear for Catholic girls. It's not sleazy or even too sophisticated. They steered clear of the Frederick's of Hollywood image of a lingerie store. They got rid of the red and made it all pink."

"So, they do a good job, right?" I ask.

"They could do better," Carol says. "One problem I have with *all* lingerie stores is that—look, here you have a section of bras. And nowadays, every bra does something a little different. It's gotten to be like cosmetics in that regard. But there's no way to know which bra does what unless you've had personal experience with it. There's no information here to explain that this bra does blah, blah, and blah. This one pushes them together, and this one shoves them up, and here's one for strapless dresses. Now, partly that is intentional. They don't want you to get too much information on your own. They'd rather even confuse you a little so that you'll take a whole bunch of bras into the dressing room, because the more you take in, they know, the better the chance that you'll buy multiple items. They've measured this, and they're right. But at the same time, it frustrates consumers."

Carol is right about that: There's no communication here, no sign that says, for example, "If you've always loved this kind of bra, you'll probably love this new style, too." Maybe there could even be an informational display telling a young woman how to build a proper lingerie wardrobe. Like, you'll need one of these and two of those and here's how to choose these little thingies.

"Women pick up their knowledge of cosmetics and lingerie in a totally ad hoc way," Carol says. "You see something about push-up bras in a magazine, or your older sister lends you her new lip gloss, and you kind of piece your information together like that."

"It's like locker room conversation."

"Right. You see somebody else try it, and you ask a few questions . . ."

"The same way adolescents learn about sex. You read three issues of *Cosmo,* and then a fifteen-year-old tells you the rest."

We've made it all the way up to the second level of the mall. We've broken out of that little cluster of stores serving young female sexuality. But we're now looking into a den of older female sexuality—the threshold of a fancy department store's fragrance section. Department stores always put the fragrance section at the entrance.

"Is this positioning a good idea or bad, do you think?" I ask.

"Bad. The thing about fine fragrance is that people buy it twice a year."

"Christmas . . ."

". . . and Mother's Day. Maybe Valentine's Day, too, although men are much less confident buying perfume than women are."

"Tell me what you think of that," I say, nodding toward the huge poster above the counter. It shows a brooding, sulky-lipped hunk, a stud of maybe twenty-one or so, with hairless, highly sculpted pectoral muscles on prominent display.

"It doesn't do anything for me," Carol says. "He's the son of the consumer, not the man she's going to bed with. I bet he's a good fifteen years younger than the average shopper in this section. I mean, put Harrison Ford up there, not this twenty-year-old. He's a *boy*. This is the Madison Avenue mentality at work. Some creatives and executives in an ad agency dream this up and cast it and style it and shoot it without bothering to understand the consumer—the person who will have to look at it. They imagine how the picture will look in the ad in *Vanity Fair* or on TV, without considering how it will play in the store. They may want to target a younger consumer. They feel that the way to do this is with a new men's fragrance geared toward this beautiful young man. They hope they'll bring a younger woman to the counter to buy this new fragrance for her young man, and then she'll shop the cosmetics, too."

"Won't that work?"

"Look around."

Ouch. Department stores' core shoppers *are* getting old, and no young women are taking their place.

"Also, men anywhere near fragrance or cosmetics is a nonstarter."

"Same for lingerie?" I ask.

"Nearly as bad."

"Apparel?"

"About the same."

"If a man is uncomfortable hanging around in the perfume aisle or shopping the racks of undergarments, is he likely to buy there?" I ask.

"I don't see how he could."

"I wonder what would happen if, say, Victoria's Secret were to open a ministore just for male shoppers at Christmas or Valentine's Day. It might look a lot like the store now does. But it would work differently," I say. "It would have to actually address size and function, and in a completely new way. Women know their sizes, and so it's no great trick to handle that when they're shopping for themselves."

"A woman knows her man's sizes, but men don't know women's, do they?"

"Men don't even know their *own* sizes," I say. "Remember, we saw men's underwear being sold to women in Filene's. Can you imagine finding women's underwear for sale in a men's clothing store? Years ago, one of our video cameras caught a guy shopping the underwear rack when he suddenly twisted around, pulled out his waistband in back and attempted to read the size on the label. It's conceivable that in his entire life he had never before bought his own underwear—first his mother bought it, then his girlfriends, now his wife."

"Can you imagine a woman not knowing what size panties she wears?" Carol says.

"Unimaginable."

"Anyway, you can see how men might feel ill at ease buying lingerie for women. For starters, he doesn't know her size. I guess if he was really intent on buying her something intimate, he could always snoop around in her dresser drawer and read a few labels."

"True," I say, "but that requires some forethought. Plus, it sounds perverted. If he gets caught, she may think he's looking for something lacy to wear under his Dockers. How would you handle ladies' lingerie for the impulse gift buy? It's February 13, and he's in a panic. He's already been to the jewelry store and didn't find anything he liked in his price range. He's prowling the mall like a desperate animal. Time is running out. Suddenly he notices a display window filled with lingerie. The lightbulb goes on—for what a modest piece of jewelry costs, he can get something truly extravagant in the fancy underwear department."

"If only he knew her size," Carol says. "It's tragic."

"What do you suggest?"

"He can say to the saleswoman, 'She's around your height . . .' "

"Or, 'Gee, I think her breasts are a little bigger than yours.' "

"Or, 'Hmm, let me hold your butt a second so I can figure out if she's a medium or a large.' "

"That might be beyond what most salesclerks are willing to abide, even those working on commission," I say.

"How about if they had mannequins of various sizes?"

"And a bunch of male customers lined up, fondling them? I don't see that, either. Maybe a gift certificate works best here."

"Or maybe at gift time the window display is dominated by garments where size is easiest—robes instead of bras."

"Anything sheer," I say.

"Or black leather," Carol says.

"The point is that it's possible to make women's merchandise easier for men to buy. And that doing so around the romance-friendly holidays might not be a bad idea. I think if men walked by Victoria's Secret and saw that some of the signs and posters and photographs were directed specifically at them, they'd feel more welcome. Just something that says, 'Sir, we'd love to show you a few perfect gifts for her.' Because right now that entire store announces, 'Hey, buddy, stay the hell out of here.' "

"It's true," she says. "You don't see many men in there, do you?"

"Sure don't. And the few who are here are all just tagging along with wives or girlfriends, with their eyes cast downward in case they accidentally see something. They're ashamed! Look at that one pathetic little chair in front of the pillar, up by the register. That's the entire accommodation for men who end up inside the store. It looks like a punishment—like the dunce chair. Merely by sitting there, a man announces, 'I am an emasculated husband waiting uncomfortably for my wife to find a thong in her size.' Especially in a mall store, where you know the woman is likely to be with her family, you've got to plan for the nonshopper as much as the shopper. A Victoria's Secret on a city street, where the typical customer is a woman on her lunch break, can get away with neglecting the needs of men and children. A mall store cannot."

"But this mall does have areas where people who aren't shopping can just sit and wait or read the paper or watch everybody else, doesn't it?" Carol says.

"Sure it does. But think about the way it works in real life. The couple is walking along when suddenly it hits her that she needs underwear. Here are her choices. She can ask him to come inside the store with her. Or, she can run in alone and leave him standing out here cooling his heels in front of a window populated by panties and bras, which means that every window shopper who passes will be staring straight at him, too. He'll love that. Or, he can find another store to go and browse, assuming there's anything he finds remotely interesting in the immediate vicinity. Maybe there is a record store or bookstore or the new Apple computer store or something like that. But most malls now group merchandise categories, meaning the women's clothing store is probably surrounded by other shops of interest to women. So he's screwed. He could go all the way down the corridor and around the corner to the public seating area. But he may not even know it's there, and secondly, she's assured him she'll just be two minutes, and so he's got to ask himself if it's worth his while to go so far to kill a hundred and twenty seconds. If there was a small waiting area just outside the store, he'd probably go there. But then you run the risk that you'll have a gaggle of guys loitering outside the lingerie store, which isn't the most agreeable setting for female push-up bra shoppers. I think that lingerie stores should do more to make males feel at ease."

"I disagree completely," Carol says. "No woman in her right mind wants to come into this store with her husband and children. This is not the kind of thing you want to be shopping for where your guy or, even worse, your eight-year-old son, can watch. You're in here to create a little romantic fantasy starring yourself, and it doesn't involve somebody's lumpy husband or bratty kids whining to go to the food court. I think it's smart of them to make it difficult for men to loiter in here, and I bet they did it as a conscious decision."

That's a good point. It runs completely counter to all that we've learned about the science of shopping, and yet I am convinced that maybe she's on to something. We once studied a store that sold dishes and tabletops and so on. We saw that many women came in with their husbands, but the men got bored tagging along, and, as a result, the women seemed pressured. The store tried adding products men might browse—bar items like cocktail shakers, shot glasses, and so on. When that happened, the men went off on their own, and total shopping time for couples rose. Sales rose, too.

But perhaps what's right for dishes is totally *wrong* for lingerie. Maybe the woman wants to tell her husband and kids to get lost for fifteen minutes, and going into Victoria's Secret is a good way to do so.

A recent study of how men and women differ when it comes to the mall turned up this fact: Men, once you get them in the door, are much more interested in the social aspect of malls than the shopping part, whereas women say the social aspect is important but shopping comes first. Men enjoy the mall as a form of recreation—they like watching people and browsing around in stores more than shopping. Maybe they'll spend fifteen minutes in a bookstore or a stereo store and leave without buying a thing. They treat it like an information-gathering trip. Men also like the nonretail parts—the rock-climbing walls, the food courts, anything that doesn't actually require them to enter stores and look at, try on, or buy merchandise. Women, of course, are there for *exactly* those things. The only females who truly love the nonshopping aspects of the mall are teenage girls. They love shopping, of course, but they also love the food courts and video arcades and all that stuff, too. And that's probably because the mall is the only nonhome, nonschool environment they have. But they outgrow that by the time they're in college. From then on, they're at malls to shop.

"Let's get back to where to put fragrance if we want men to buy it," I say.

"In Sears near the power tools?"

"I bet more men would buy it there than in the cosmetics department."

"Where else?"

"Closer to jewelry might work," I say. "In fact, you could group all the traditional gifts that men give women and see how that works. That's one of the few remaining advantages this department store has over a specialty shop or boutique—that wide range of merchandise. They can get a little creative with their juxtapositions."

"So you'd have fragrance, jewelry, and lingerie all together, in a way that feels male-accessible," Carol says.

"Yeah. You'd put up graphics showing a man making a purchase of something gift-wrapped with a pink bow. With that big hint, at least some men might be psychologically able to enter the area and shop it. Put a salesclerk at the entrance to guide men across the threshold—a good-looking woman to take him by the arm and gently drag him inside. And I think women would be willing to buy things there, too."

"The Extravagance Shop."

"Right. I'd give it a name to appeal to guys. It would give them permission to shop there, something men really don't have now in women's departments. And I'd make sure it was marketed to male shoppers, especially around the usual gift times like Christmas, Valentine's Day. . . ."

"Yes," says Carol. "Because fragrance only gets shopped twice a year, having it at the entrance gives the impression that the store is empty."

"It is less crowded there than anywhere else, but is that a bad thing?"

"Sure, who wants to shop at a store where nobody goes? It's like going into an empty restaurant. It doesn't inspire great confidence."

"Do you know why fragrance is traditionally right inside the entrance in department stores?" I say. "Because, back in the days before cars, the perfume section was a bulwark against the stench of horse manure coming in from the street."

"Fascinating," says Carol.

Sounds like Carol's had her fill of the mall, considering that today's her day off and she spends plenty of work time in shopping centers anyway. It's an occupational hazard, mall-sickness, one even I've experienced. Time to move on.

9 *The Charmin Challenge*

I NEED TO use the bathroom, and you're coming with me.

From the developers' point of view, this particular amenity is a necessary evil. If you're going to invite people to your mall, not to mention your food court, you've got to give them toilets. You don't have a choice. This may sound like a callous attitude—and it is—but it's also easy to understand. It's a real cost and effort to keep public bathrooms presentable.

Bathrooms are nothing but trouble. Years ago, some mall men's rooms were notorious as gay trysting stations, particularly ones located within department stores. It's less of an issue today. One wise developer I know always locates the manager's office near the johns, on the theory that employees will therefore be more likely to check in on the facility from time to time. I can't say whether it makes a bit of difference.

You can just imagine the insurance and legal liability issues that arise. To the extent that muggings do occur in malls, they may take place in rest rooms, which are usually hidden down some lonesome corridor away from the main thoroughfare. In fact, that's the best way to find the bathroom in an unfamiliar mall—look around for the least inviting hallway, the narrow one where the lighting is dimmest.

See? Here's just such a passage radiating off the promenade. It's gloomy and unwelcoming—if the mall were an urban setting, this would be an alley. Come on, let's go inside.

This is the typical mall bathroom—institutional tile and porcelain in neutral shades. At least it's clean, and it appears there are paper towels in the dispensers.

It's always striking how planners of big public places such as malls, sports arenas, concert halls, and so on mishandle the gender differential in bathrooms. Just stand out in the corridor and count the number of people walking in the rest room doors. You'll learn an important fact that architects seem never to realize.

Women use the bathroom more than men. They spend more time in them, too. These must be little-understood truths; otherwise, there would be twice as many ladies' bathrooms as men's, or the former would be double the size of the latter. But they're not. Planners are rigidly symmetrical where bathrooms are concerned. It's why, for instance, you often see a line outside the ladies' room but rarely at the gents'.

When you consider how much the mall depends on the goodwill of its female market base in particular, you can see how the number and condition of bathrooms might be somewhat important. As we've seen elsewhere, the critical issue for mall owners is finding ways to extend the average visit. Talk to any woman and you quickly learn how pleasant bathrooms make prolonged visits possible, while nasty toilets encourage the quick in-and-out.

*   *   *

Not only do women use rest rooms more often than men do, but they require more once there. Is it any surprise that male mall executives might not always provide for the most pleasant breast-feeding experience? It isn't, but that's one of the added functions I'm talking about, and an important one considering how happy many mothers of young children are to take advantage of a mall's distractions.

I admire any mall, department store, or other retailer that pays attention to the lowly toilet, for that is a company building goodwill. There are so few good public facilities in America that firms which provide them will stand out. If you walk the streets of New York today, there are only a few reliable bathroom stops you can make: most hotel lobbies, and, for some reason, any Barnes & Noble. Even their men's rooms feature baby changing tables, which exhibits a sure knowledge of customer habits, since so many urbane dads take the little ones out for a stroll to the nearest bookstore. The bathrooms designed by Philippe Starck for the Delano and Paramount Hotels are so distinctive that they've become required stops for tourists. Still, most public places—malls included—go on treating this most necessary and human place as something shameful.

But at least the mall can be counted on to provide a bathroom of some sort. Retailers and even fast-food restaurants have seen fit to phase out this particular amenity, which strikes me as a heartless disregard for their customers' humanity and dignity. But they save a lot of dough and aggravation. The other day I was in a Starbucks in New York when a customer asked for the rest room. She had a French accent, and so, I assume, she had grown up under the misguided notion that businesses selling beverages make some accommodation for nature's call.

"We don't have bathrooms," the *barista* said, then added helpfully: "Try the diner on the corner—*they* have bathrooms."

Maybe it's just in the United States that we're so weird about washing and changing and going to the bathroom? In some Japanese stores and malls, you'll find freestanding sinks located outside of the bathrooms, permitting shoppers who need only to wash their hands a way to do so without crowding the johns. It is also a public statement about hygiene as an important issue. That's a smart move, but not surprising in a culture where bathing has an exalted role in the average person's life. (Some Japanese public toilets are equipped with bidets.)

What always amazes me as I stand in this spot is that the mall, which is a temple to blandishment and consumption, can't think of a single interesting thing to do with a bathroom. Here you've got a captive audience, one that will probably spend at least sixty seconds or so with nothing much to see or hear. And the mall does zero to fill those empty moments.

What would a more enterprising mind do? Well, the simplest solution would be to sell some advertising positions—maybe a few poster spots over the urinals, or on the inside of stall doors, or above the sinks. That's the obvious answer.

The rest room could be turned over to one of the several shops in the mall selling bath-related products, such as soap, skin cream, fragrance, hair care. Your average mall bathroom's ambience would be dramatically improved if, say, Aveda or The Body Shop furnished the sinks with samples of various sweet-smelling goods. Even cosmetics would work here—women love trying the newest lipstick or fragrance. A woman could test some new soap or moisturizer, want more, and be directed to the store to find it. A guy could discover some new hair gel or virile cologne and do likewise. Or there could be monitors showing promotional fashion videos or new DVD releases from the music store. The acoustics in here would be awesome with a decent sound system.

Not long ago I toured a new prototype store for Lowe's, the home improvement chain, with maybe ten members of the senior marketing team. At some point I asked to see the ladies' room, which caused a certain amount of unease among my all-male companions, but we found a woman to enter first to check if the coast was clear, and in we went. The first shock came when a quick poll of the group revealed that not one of these men had ever been in a ladies' room, despite their high position and years of service at a company that depends on female customer satisfaction practically above all else. The second revelation was that the bathroom, while clean and odorless, was also the most generic, no-frills facility imaginable—kind of weird, I pointed out, in a store that tries hard to convince people to buy modern, luxurious bathrooms.

"Has no one ever considered using this as a kind of showroom for the things you sell out there on the floor of the store, twenty-five feet away?" I asked. "What if you turned each bathroom over to a different manufacturer?" I asked. "This could be the American Standard rest room, and they would install all their coolest sinks and toilets here, and maybe Kohler could redo the men's room, and so on like that."

I've suggested to the marketing people at Proctor & Gamble that they sponsor ladies' rooms in major airports—hire an attendant with a mop and a bucket to keep the place clean, and stock the joint with all their newest products. They could, in each stall, offer some no-frills brand of toilet paper alongside the latest, plushest innovation from Charmin—a comparison test at least as compelling as the Pepsi challenge. It isn't an outlandish proposal—if the magic bullet in twenty-first-century marketing is creating buzz, the bathroom at the airport has the right demographics, enough anxiety to ensure that most people's personal radar systems are up and running, and the assurance that whatever the impression—it's going somewhere.

The fact that no bathroom to my knowledge does any of this—and I make a point of visiting the rest rooms on every mall trip—is but one more example of the usual disconnect between the real estate–minded management and the building's function as one great big retailing machine. An entrepreneurial approach to the well-appointed rest room could turn even this place into a profit center.

10 Status Anxiety and Back Pockets

WE'RE about to plunge into another shopping expedition. We have a seemingly straightforward task before us—finding jeans for Michelle. But as is usually the case in the mall, nothing is as simple as it seems.

We're going to meet Michelle near the Ralph Lauren store, which is as good a landmark as any. She is a twenty-year-old who hails from Staten Island. She has an Irish father and Palestinian mother, giving her a lovely olive complexion and a wit more mature than her years. She has a very precise style, no unusual piercings, no visible tattoos. Her eyebrows are neatly manicured, and occasionally the makeup gets a little dramatic.

Staten Island is a New York City borough separated from the rest of the world by three bridges and a ferry. It has a short subway, a small greenbelt, and a Tibetan art museum that more outsiders than locals know about. Staten Island weddings are famous for the pastel colors of the dresses and dinner jackets of the bridesmaids and ushers. Parts of it are grimy and industrial, but the side that faces New York Harbor has some of the most spectacular views on the eastern seaboard. The Verrazano Narrows Bridge linking Staten Island with Brooklyn has a $9 toll, making it an expensive trip to the mainland. It is home to mobsters and hardworking immigrants making the transition from urban to suburban life. Historically, the only reason to leave is to work or to visit Yankee Stadium, and now that Staten Island has its own minor league baseball club, there is even less reason to wander.

Michelle gets up before dawn to make the ninety-minute commute to her job in Manhattan. Twice a month she'll go clubbing there on a weekend night. Through her job and her excursions, she's seen the world beyond her island. As the product of a blue-collar family in a pink-collar job, she is growing in white-collar directions. Her aspirations and appetites are as boundless as her pocketbook is limited. She lives at home, and a big piece of her paycheck is devoted to car payments. She has definitely outgrown her teenage years. She knows the names of some famous English DJs, giggles at *Cosmo,* and can spot (or thinks she can) a fake Hermès bag at twenty-five paces. She knows about classic good looks and works hard to present herself.

To Michelle, our mall is nirvana. To get there she has to drive past at least three other major shopping centers, but she'll make this trip two or three times a year.

And here she is, right on time.

"Michelle, how far are we from your home?"

"Hmm, maybe twenty-five minutes if there's no traffic."

"So it's not really far. But this isn't your usual mall, is it?"

"No, there are two other malls where we'd normally go."

" 'We' meaning?"

"Me and my girlfriends."

She's here alone today.

"Why *do* you come here?" I ask.

"It's got some nicer stores that the other malls don't have. There's a Diesel and an Armani Exchange here. This is where you come when you know what you're looking for. This isn't a browsing mall for us."

"What does that mean? Why wouldn't you come here to browse?"

"Because everything here is more expensive than at the other malls. And it's farther away."

"Got it. If you were here with your friends, would you all drive separately?"

"No, together."

We're walking past a department store when we see a sign announcing the presence of Georg Jensen silver.

"What do you think of this sign here?" I ask.

"I have no idea what it means."

"Do you know the name Georg Jensen?"

"I wish I did, because it makes me feel a little ignorant to see a sign like that and have no clue what it's about."

"It's a Scandinavian silver maker. Just a brand name, like Ralph Lauren."

"Actually," she says, "I went into the Ralph Lauren store while I was waiting for you."

"Did you look at jeans?"

"No, I felt invisible there."

"What?"

"Because nobody seemed to notice me, not even the salesclerks."

"So you left."

"Of course."

"Is there something intimidating to you about this mall?"

"Sort of."

"Can you describe it?"

"Well, you walk in, I don't know . . . if I go into Saks, I don't feel like anyone thinks I'm going to be a big spender, so they don't care enough to ask me how I'm doing, or if I found my size or anything like that. I even get the same feeling about the people who shop in the mall. That they're all kind of snooty, and so the people who work in the stores are, too. Or they want to be snooty."

We enter a fashionable young women's apparel retailer.

"Have you been in this store before?"

"Yeah."

"Ever bought anything?"

"No."

The slender and attractive sales associate comes over.

"Hi, how are you?"

"Good," says Michelle.

"Fine," say I.

Michelle has barely begun examining jeans when she has a question.

"Do you have any with back pockets?"

"No, we don't."

"None?"

"No."

Michelle turns to go.

"What's the deal with the pockets?"

"I only wear jeans with back pockets."

"Only?"

"Yeah."

"Why?"

"Because the ones without pockets don't look right on me."

"You like the pockets?"

"I like how they look."

"Would you ever put anything in them?"

"It's not about what you put in them."

"So you *wouldn't* put anything in them?"

"Oh, maybe if I was going out and I didn't wear a jacket and didn't want to carry around a bag, I'd put some cash and my license in the back pocket. . . ."

"Not a wallet?"

"No!"

"A cell phone?"

"Very funny."

"So what's the point of the pockets, then?"

"Pockets makes the difference in how they're made. And usually jeans without pockets are stretch, and I don't like how stretch jeans look on me."

"It has something to do with how they look in back, I'm getting that sense, am I right?"

"Yes," she says patiently. "If you're really skinny, then it doesn't matter, but I'm not skinny back there. So it matters."

How did I know it was headed back there? Somehow, when shopping for women's clothes, it invariably comes down to the butt. No wonder there's such dizzying variety in the world of jeans, meant as they are to display (to good or ill) that part of their wearer, male or female. Jeans are also the uniform of the mall, regardless of the age of the wearer. I've made the point that we come to the mall to satisfy our need to watch people, but I'd wager that, after faces, the most popular focus for our looking is the butt. Most of those butts being watched are female, because women scrutinize them as avidly as men do, albeit for different reasons.

"How often do you sell a pair of jeans to someone over thirty?" I ask the associate.

"Every day."

"How about over forty?"

"I sold a pair this morning to a woman around seventy-five."

"They were for her granddaughter, though."

"No, they were for her."

"Did she look good in them?"

"They looked nice."

Next we come upon Diesel, the weirdly named, high-style Italian sportswear store.

There are plenty of jeans inside, displayed in a prominent and extremely confusing exhibit front and center in the store. You can't even tell which are women's and which are men's. In addition, the variations are dizzying—the fit, the shape of the leg, the coloration, on and on.

"Do you think these jeans are for guys or girls?"

"I think these are guys'."

An employee has ambled over to listen in.

"What makes you say that?" I ask.

"These look a little feminine. But those definitely look masculine."

"You're probably right. But do you notice how often this kind of confusion happens in clothing stores today?"

"It happens to me all the time. At the Gap especially, but anyplace where they sell men's and women's clothes next to each other. It happens at the sneaker store even, until you begin to pick out the pink trim."

This is a real issue for retailers, finding a way to signal gender to shoppers. You'd think that knowing which garments are for which sex would be the easiest thing in the world. I'll bet that back in the 1950s no one ever anticipated a world where clothing for adults of both sexes was sold side by side, and you'd have trouble telling one from the other. This is where graphics, especially big photographs, come in handy. It's an obvious solution, but fairly foolproof.

"Can I help you?" the associate asks at last.

"Yeah," I say, "what are we looking at?"

"Well, uh, these up this side are for men, and these down here are for women."

"Are you conscious that this is deliberately confusing?" I am referring to the fact that Diesel executives freely admit that they design confusing displays on purpose, based on the principle that a shopper who requires sales assistance is more likely to buy than one who shops solo. This is a truism in the world of shopping, by the way, and so quite possibly this decision was a clever one. Smart retailers are always trying to figure out ways to get shoppers to talk to their employees. The most obvious means, the no-brainer method, is what's known as "the six-second greeting" (or, in slower environments, "the ten-second greeting"), which simply dictate that a clerk will address a shopper within six (or ten) seconds of entering the store. The question then is what happens after that hearty, "Hi, howyadointoday!" In too many stores, the answer is "nothing"—nobody's bothered to figure it out all the way.

"But that's frustrating," Michelle says. "What if you want to buy jeans, but all the help is busy with other customers? And you just want to pick out a pair of jeans and go?"

"Well, the company doesn't believe that most shoppers will self-buy a pair of $150 jeans. So they make it all but impossible to pick anything without help from a clerk," I say. "They make it confusing—"

"Well," interjects the clerk, "it's not actually confusing, but—"

"No, I've read interviews with Diesel executives," I interrupt her right back. "They say it's confusing."

"Okay, I guess it is. But only the first few times you shop here."

This just deepens the sensation that you have to become a Diesel person—that you go through stages, from being ignorant to being somewhat knowledgeable to being a member of the club, which imparts a cultlike status. Which, again, is not a bad thing.

"Okay, can you take us through this?"

"Sure," the associate says, now turning her gaze on Michelle. "What you do is look at the picture and tell me what you like, and I can locate the style for you on the wall over here," she says, gesturing toward the built-in shelving that goes from floor to ceiling. "Do you know if you're looking for a low rise, a high rise?"

"Not too low. But not too high."

"A medium rise. Do you like boot cut? You're wearing boot-cut jeans."

"Yes. What color do they come in?"

"That style comes in the mocha, the copper, the green wash, that dark wash down there. . . ."

"Do they have a back pocket?"

"Uh . . . no. Do you like this color?"

"Not without a back pocket, I don't."

We head for another store.

"Michelle, let's check for back pockets first, okay?"

She rummages through the first denim display we hit.

"Pockets!"

We can relax a little now. The trail's getting warm.

"Hi, can I help you?"

"Do you have these in my size?" Michelle asks. The sales associate leads us over to a rack of jeans, all of which have back pockets, only now there's another issue to be considered.

"Michelle," I say, "whiskers or no?"

"Huh?"

"Whiskers. Those lines that make jeans look worn-in."

"Right. Whiskers, yes."

"Yes?"

"Why would they be a no?"

"No, I'm just wondering why they're a yes."

"They're cute. They look broken in. It's like new vintage jeans."

"True. But what's interesting about whiskers is where they bring the eye. We used to think jeans were only about the butt—how they fit back there. That still counts, only now *this* is the focus, too—the front. Whiskers draw your eye to the front."

"I guess they do!"

"Would you feel comfortable wearing jeans with whiskers if you were a guy?"

"You know," Michelle says, "until you mentioned it, I never thought about it."

"Or, if you see a guy wearing jeans with whiskers, do your eyes immediately go there?"

"I'll have to start paying attention."

"What is this guy talking about?" the associate asks her.

"Oh, nothing," Michelle says.

"My name is Melissa," she says directly to Michelle. "If you need any help, feel free to ask."

Michelle turns and waves to me. "Thanks, I'll take it from here."

11 *Fun*

I'M BORED.

Luckily, this mall offers quite a few things that have nothing to do with shopping. There must be a lot of people bored with shopping, since the nonstore portion of malls—what is sometimes optimistically referred to as the "entertainment"—keeps becoming a bigger part of the mix. Once upon a time, a dank little video game arcade was considered sufficient. Today malls have taken on a lot of the burden of keeping suburban America diverted.

In truth, the nonstore aspects are the only things that give a mall its character, since the stores are essentially identical from one mall to another. So far today here's what we've encountered:

A rock-climbing wall.

An ice rink. (For some reason, there was a spell when it seemed as if every mall in Texas was getting an ice rink. Do so many Texans really care to skate, or is it just that big Texas personality expressing itself by bringing rinks to areas where the temperature often tops a hundred degrees?)

A food court, of course. And that doesn't even take into account all the other shops and stands here where you can buy something to eat. All this food is meant for immediate gratification, too. Unlike malls abroad, ours rarely feature much in the way of real prepared food meant to be taken home and consumed. And malls here rarely include supermarkets. Mall eats are invariably low-fiber, high-sugar, high-fat, tasty, and fast. And there's food in your face every time you turn around.

A movie theater. But a movie feels like a treat after a day's shopping, not something you do in the middle of the afternoon. (Although just knowing that Jackie Chan movie is playing right now makes me a little antsy.)

And still awaiting us is the uppermost level of the mall. Reportedly, it is vast and given over to the amusement of adolescents and the young at heart (meaning middle-aged men who get as antsy as teenagers elsewhere in the mall).

The fact that malls keep increasing the amount of space they devote to nonshopping functions would indicate that there must be some economic sense to it. The thinking is simply that these various amusements extend the amount of time people will spend here. They do so in two ways. First, by supplying more than just a place to shop. This is a sound thought. If you've managed to attract people here for one purpose, you ought to see if there are other desires you can fulfill. It's fine if they come to shop, even better if they shop and eat, better than that if they shop, eat, play, socialize, and so on. This principle extends throughout retailing, not just here. If a convenience store can get you inside to buy milk, will you also stay to microwave a burrito?

It's been proven that the more time someone spends in a mall, the more stores they visit and the more things they buy. Again, there's an inescapable logic to that formula. Every mall owner in the world knows all this. It's just that they respond differently to it. Some like the idea of putting in a big, glitzy, raucous entertainment sector. It's the expensive way to go, but it's easy, too—you just install it and turn on the lights.

Entertainment also prolongs the stay by solving the central problem of group shopping: What do we do with the nonshopper? If an adult has to drag two sullen adolescents along for every step of a shopping expedition, you can be sure that the trip will end prematurely. Whereas if those adolescents can be given some enjoyable outlet for their energies, they'll let you shop for as long as you want. The mere promise of a reward may keep them quiet. (Of course, when you're ready to go you may have to drag them *out* of the mall.) This is the mall as suburban baby-sitter. You can force small children to go where you want, but once they wise up they present challenges. Taking them to the mall may seem safer than leaving them home, and sending them with a few bucks off to the arcade, food court, or movie is saner than keeping them by your side.

But the connection between such amusements and increased spending isn't ironclad. People may now come to the mall without intending to buy a single thing. In a recent study, slightly more than half of what people did in malls was unrelated to actual shopping—eating, movies, games, hanging out, socializing, and so on. Those who said the primary reason they came to the mall was "to have fun" spent less money than those who said they came to visit a department store—to *shop*. The survey also found that the overall perceived entertainment value of a mall is unrelated to the amount of time people devote to shopping or the number of items they buy. So shoppers can be exceedingly fond of their mall and still not spend much money or time in stores. It's a risk.

Malls sometimes err by placing the entertainment functions too far away from everything else. There's a certain logic to keeping the video game fans away from the devoted shoppers. But it's awfully easy to reach the entertainment cluster of this mall without having to pass many store windows. Perhaps the landlord should disrupt that smooth traffic pattern and force people to work their way through the mall before reaching this level. It might even make sense to put stores that appeal to teenagers—music, certain apparel stores, Spencer Gifts—either up here or at the base of the escalator leading here.

Teenage girls love malls best, I think—and here, according to a survey, is what they say they want in malls: a hangout-type Internet café–coffee shop (the kind of slacker paradise you find in cities, usually peopled with unemployed dot-commers); movie theaters; big seat-ing/socializing areas; places that boys might like; amusements, such as Ferris wheels and so on; and sports, including bowling alleys, batting cages, miniature golf, tennis. It's a long list.

One teenage girl tried to describe what would be in her perfect mall.

"I don't know if you've even been to Washington Square in New York," she began, "but it's this park, and they have these tables with like built-in checkerboards on top?"

These kids crave cities—they want to be a part of the human spec-tacle that exists whenever people come together. Sadly, what we've given them instead is malls. So the mall should attempt to provide some of the things that make adolescent society possible and enjoy-able.

Even stores can serve as forms of entertainment. Here's one cate-gory that's vanishing from malls overall, but can still occasionally be found: pet shops. Selling critters in the mall looks like a labor-intensive, somehow seedy undertaking. Still, go to any mall pet store, and you'll find children gathered around the front windows or the cages inside. It's like a zoo for small domestic animals—puppies, kittens, bunnies, the occasional piglet, all romping inside their too-small cages. It's one of those places parents dread. But five or ten minutes in such a store can restore the spirits of a cranky seven-year-old, thereby making it possible for parents to shop a little longer. Thanks to Animal Planet and the Discovery Channel, we get visually close to animals, but we can't smell or touch them. Even the modern zoo is discovering that close-ness to simple domesticated critters like goats, sheep, and ponies is a major draw.

Okay, here we are—the top level of the mall. It's crowded and bustling with high adolescent spirits and good energy as the teenagers bop from one video game to the next. There's a noticeable absence of shopping bags in their hands—these are not your prime shoppers. But that's not why they're here. The music is techno and loud. Over on one side is the food court, which faces the Ferris wheel. That's a good idea, considering how most food courts give you nothing to look at. It's also interesting to note that the only window in the food court is way up at the top of the Ferris wheel, meaning riders get a pretty cool view of the surrounding countryside. That's better than the celebrated new Ferris wheel inside Toys "R" Us's Times Square store, which affords only a view of the ceiling.

There's something that looks like the NASCAR wing of the mall up here—lots of driving video games and racing paraphernalia for sale. And it's mobbed, of course. Back behind that is the ice rink, and there's some kind of restaurant up here, it's a hybrid, part eating place, part playground. It actually has an old-fashioned tabletop shuffleboard set up, with sawdust and hanging lamp and everything.

And in back of the restaurant, maybe the purest entertainment chamber in the entire mall—a deafening, throbbing, clanging, whistling hall filled with every type of video game imaginable, including one in which you slam drums along to karaoke-style music. At some of the games you can win prizes, and under one teenage girl's seat is a long snake of tickets—there must be hundreds of them. This room feels like hell on earth to anyone over twenty-five, which means it's like Mecca for your average adolescent.

A few steps farther down the hallway, there's a large space that must have been devoted to something or other, once upon a time. Right now it's being used by two little guys for a Frisbee match. As garish and crazed as it feels up here, it makes a kind of sense. They've taken an entire level of the mall and essentially created a place where most adults wouldn't want to go. If they do come up here, believe me, they're not staying long. But it reinforces the concept of the mall as a destination with many purposes—like a city, in that regard. It goes from being a place for shoppers to one where the entire family can enjoy some of its leisure. Parents can shop and eat down there, and the kids can play, eat, ride the Ferris wheel, and so on up here. Having the kids' level up top makes perfect sense—parents can relax a little knowing that their children are upstairs, farther from the outside world.

12 *Hands-Free Shopping*

MY HANDS are full.

If you've been paying attention, you know that I haven't actually purchased anything, and so my hands are as free as they were when I entered. But if I were a normal mall shopper, chances are by now I'd have bought *something*.

Depending on the weather outside and how far I parked from the entrance, I might also be carrying around my coat. If I had children along, I'd probably end up carrying their coats, too.

As part of the Envirosell playbook, what shoppers do with their hands is a critical issue. Whether you're stroking cashmere sweaters, hefting portable CD players or opening doors, your hands are key.

Some stores try to accommodate this fact of human physiology by providing handbaskets or shopping carts, which makes life quite a bit easier, especially if you're serious about buying something. We've done quite a few studies that bear this out, one way or another. Stores that offer baskets sell more than those that don't. And when stores increase the size of the baskets, they often find that shoppers purchase more items.

Many urban stores, as a security measure, ask shoppers to leave bags and briefcases with a guard just inside the entrance. This does decrease shoplifting as intended, but there's also an unintended benefit—it frees up the shoppers' hands, thus allowing them to scoop up more merchandise on their way to the checkout line.

If keeping a shopper's hands as free as possible makes a difference in a single store, you can imagine the impact in a mall, where the average person might enter a dozen shops in the course of a single expedition.

What do malls do to allow for this? Almost nothing. Once again, I believe this can be attributed to the disconnect between the real estate–driven developer and the retail-driven shopper. In a mall, space is money, and so management wants to dedicate as little space as possible to uses that don't generate profits. To be fair, you do find, in a few malls, coin-operated storage, like historically you found in bus stations and train stations. Even those were tucked away, often in the long corridor leading to the rest rooms. With the security concerns post September 11, that storage has largely disappeared.

I'm talking about coat check areas near every entrance.

I'm talking about will-call desks so that purchases can be held aside until you're ready to leave the mall.

Shopping carts to roll from store to store.

Baby strollers.

Hands-free shopping.

There are malls that offer coat checks. Typically, this service is provided by some local organization, such as the Kiwanis, who will charge a small fee and in that way raise money to fund good works. It may be admirable citizenship, but these setups always feel like amateur hour. They're usually tucked away in some underperforming corner of the mall, rather than where they should be—front and center, welcoming to every person who enters. Also, they usually handle coats and umbrellas only, which is part of the battle but far from all of it. And they don't inspire great confidence that your possessions will be competently guarded.

Ideally, every time you bought anything in the mall, the cashier would offer to run it down to the will-call desk for you, where you could retrieve it on your way out the door. In a perfect world, you might even be able to get your car first, then drive it up to the will-call exit, where a nice high school student would help you load whatever you bought into your trunk. It works at supermarkets, where some nice kid wheels your stuff out to your vehicle.

Never having to carry a purchase from one store to another (to another) and then to the bathroom and the food court and then up the rock-climbing wall would be a vast improvement over the current method, whereby you're stuck carting around whatever you bought, in whichever sequence you bought it. Even if you shop a small fraction of the 144 stores here, your burdens add up. The worst thing, from the mall's perspective, is the shopper who decides to run his or her bags out to the car. There's a chance that person will get out there and decide to go on home.

But maybe you're the kind of person who dreads coat checks and will-call desks because you fear a logjam just at the moment you want to leave. Plenty of people have an aversion to valet parking for the same reason.

In your case, the mall could offer shopping carts. Some shopping centers have experimented with them, but they have yet to catch on. Shopping carts are redolent of supermarkets, which feels a little low-rent to some mall operators and retailers. They're uncomfortable with the thought of tossing your brand new DKNY skirt into something better suited to carrying Cheerios. By contrast, many European malls have successfully and stylishly integrated supermarkets into the mall and thus shopping carts as well.

There *are* elegant shopping carts to be had—baskets riding atop silent rubber tires, with maybe a hanging rack for garments. Given the overall casual style of the mall itself, it doesn't seem as though carts would automatically be an aesthetic violation. Malls are now courting twenty-first century anchor tenants like the giant discounter Target. One of their criteria is whether shopping carts are welcomed, not just in the mall but in the parking garage or lot, too. More than one Target deal has been kiboshed by shopping cart–garage conflicts.

CALL OF THE MALL

There's never a shortage of baby strollers in the mall, because parents feel free to bring them along. Still, it can be a hassle—you've got to unload the kids and the stroller and get the whole procession inside from the lot or garage. If an elevator trip is involved, it becomes even more cumbersome, especially on weekends when the mall is crowded. It's a temptation to leave the stroller in the minivan, except then the adult shoppers will be constrained by the endurance of small children, who can become tired and cranky without warning.

All this sounds like common sense, and yet malls make little accommodation for it. Some do provide strollers—but they, too, are usually hidden away in some corner, and almost always cost a few bucks to rent for the day. This seems about as sensible as charging people to use a shopping cart—making pennies off what, if offered free, would generate dollars.

13 Pushcarts Rule

HEY, WHAT'S this up ahead? Hold on a second.

I don't really need automatic gutter cleaners. I live on the first floor of an apartment building. And yet I am slightly fascinated by this little booth here—a pushcart, almost—right in the middle of the corridor, the one with the slightly bored-looking woman demonstrating for any-one who cares to watch (just me) how a gizmo can clear all the wet leaves and dead birds and whatever out of your gutters, thereby spar-ing you a climb up a rickety ladder.

It's not the kind of thing you'd expect anybody to buy on impulse while walking through the mall. And yet it's here, and paying a hand-some rent no doubt, so somebody must be willing.

"How much does this thing go for?"

"Depends on your house," she says. "It starts at around $3,000."

"And do you sell any?"

"Enough," she says warily.

Maybe she thinks I'm a competitor? I'm standing here transfixed as a three-foot-long section of simulated roof gutter is swept clear by the gadget she's selling. The mall doesn't provide many guy moments, but this little demonstration has to rank among the most fascinating.

Right next to this is a more lighthearted pushcart—the bungee ball man, who spends the day showing off the coolness of his toy. It is an old pushcart profession that takes many forms. Someone takes a toy where some simple skill is involved—a ball tied to a paddle by a thick rubber band, a plastic airplane that returns to sender like a boomerang, a remote-control car—and demonstrates it. It always looks easier to master than it really is, as many customers can attest. The purchase is often as much a payment for the pleasure of watching the demonstration.

Judging by the audience he's gathered, this little vignette is a godsend. There are mostly dads and kids gathered around, no doubt happy to find something even mildly entertaining while mom goes about the serious business of acquisitioning.

It's a testament to the constantly evolving nature of the mall that most now include these freestanding kiosks. They tend to be locally owned and operated. Small-time retail, in other words, in marked contrast to the huge, slick chains that predominate in here. You may find some goods in kiosks that are sold elsewhere in the mall—costume jewelry, toys. But it's mostly the kind of merchandise that feels at home on a wooden cart plunked down right in the pedestrian path—cheap sunglasses, human-hair wigs, extravagant christening outfits, cell phones and pagers, put-your-photo-on-a-sweatshirt, celebrity posters. The "As-Seen-on-TV" shop thrives here, meaning you can buy a Hairdini braid twister even if you can never manage to jot down the 800 number before the commercial ends. Tupperware lives here, too—you can't really imagine an entire mall store devoted to plastic containers for leftovers, but it makes for a high-profile, crowd-pleasing kiosk.

When these things first began to show up in malls, tenants were outraged. The complaint was that the carts cheapened the ambience; they also were competitors who got away with paying less than the full mall rents, which didn't help their image among fellow tenants. So there was a trade-off, and even the danger that the kiosks would hurt the stores' sales, which would in turn cut into the mall developer's revenues. Still, the malls were willing to run a few risks if doing so allowed them to squeeze a few more leasable square feet out of the premises. Heretofore, the space occupied by kiosks was being used by shoppers to walk. Maybe they had more space than they needed?

At its inception, the pushcart was a brilliant retail concept. A small, efficient, mobile store, operated by one person, specializing in a few (or just one) product categories, and ideally suited to being examined by the shopper, since it is all surface and is approachable from all sides. No wonder pushcarts have been around so long, probably as long as we've had wheels.

Pushcarts were part of our retail memory, until they made their mall-related comeback. It started as a brilliant innovation at Faneuil Hall in Boston. At the time, the mall was about to open with less than a full roster of tenants. Somebody had the idea to fill in the gaps with pushcarts. They made things seem a little more bustling. The mall's developer, the Rouse Company, charged a nominal rent at first, unaware of what a dependable source of healthy income the carts would become. Since then, the classy peddler has become a signature of Rouse malls.

But then, as usually happens, the greedheads got hold of the concept and rode it for all it's worth. If you divide the mall into the smallest real estate parcels possible, you can charge a lot more money for them. Today, most malls have dedicated some portion of formerly open space to what are usually termed kiosks, in acknowledgment of the fact that rarely does anyone actually *push* these things.

From the mall's view, kiosks are wonderful for one main reason— the rents they kick in. Annual leases can hit $50,000 for a forty-five-square-foot kiosk, which is a lot more than Neiman Marcus pays, foot for foot. As much as 2 to 3 percent of a mall's total rental revenue can come from the carts. "It's real money, let's put it that way," said an executive from a developer that owns more than 150 malls. One estimate says that over 150,000 kiosks currently exist in American malls and shopping centers. They've become such a staple of retailing that now they proliferate in airports and office buildings, too.

The kiosks throw off so much easy rent (since they require no maintenance by the mall), that it's easy to overdose on them. Bring in too many and they begin to overwhelm the passageways. We use the terms "laudable crowding" and "impenetrable crowding." In the former, you're strolling through the mall and look up ahead to see an area that's bustling with genial hubbub. It makes you want to go there and see what everybody else is looking at. "Impenetrable crowding" is when you're strolling and look ahead to see a traffic jam of shoppers struggling to move. Kiosks placed too close together or jammed into inappropriate spots cause bad bustle. One look at the crowd of exasperated shoppers trying to get past and you decide to take a detour. In doing so, of course, you bypass every store in that area.

Good kiosks add something fun and even a little exotic to a mall's mix. Really good kiosks will surprise you—one of the best I ever saw was one selling microwavable heating pads. It's not that the pads themselves were so amazing, but I loved the lady who was selling them. She'd throw a few into her microwave while describing to the small crowd that invariably gathered how they worked. Once one was ready, she'd take it out and apply it to the aching neck or back of some volunteer shopper. It was a little bit of theater along with your shopping, and it harkened back to another vestige of ancient retailing—the barker.

Pushcarts are pure retailing. If you go to any store in this mall, you'll find some $40,000-a-year manager running the show, but only in the narrowest sense. In stores owned by national chains, all the big decisions about what will be sold and how, and at what price, and the way in which things will be displayed—the stuff that makes retailing an art—are made elsewhere. The kids running these shops aren't merchants by any stretch of the imagination. Whereas successful kiosk owners are working their retail magic—figuring out what works, succeeding or failing on the strength of their wit, ability, and energy.

They remind me of a produce stand I saw in a market in Istanbul. It was owned and run by an ancient man who'd probably been at it all his working life. I watched him for half an hour early one morning as he carefully positioned every apple and pear and eggplant, turning each piece in his hands to find the most perfect side, then placing it all just so on his cart. It was a work of art by the time he was through. He was no retailing titan or merchandising wizard. It was just a produce stand. But he was a merchant, top to bottom, intimately involved in every aspect of retailing, from purchasing the goods to displaying them for maximum appeal. I'm sure that his grasp of why we buy exceeds that of most mall store managers, simply because he understands and controls the process in its entirety. I don't mean to pick on mall store managers—it's not their fault that their employers expect so little of them. That's the nature of large, centralized corporations today, where all the meaningful decisions are made in a single office, by men and women who spend as little time as possible on the selling floor.

I love the Tupperware kiosk—the colorful plastic containers make for great displays, and they're just the kind of impulse purchase that does well in such a tiny space, in the midst of foot traffic. You don't need to deliberate for hours, just pick out what you need, pay, and go. I once saw a kiosk that sold only purple-colored merchandise, again, a brilliant idea from the display point of view.

Lots of kiosks specialize in goods meant for ethnic shoppers— human-hair wigs that are popular for African American women, or extravagant christening costumes that seem intended for Spanish-speaking customers, if the signage and staffing are any indication. You can't imagine these categories being able to support an entire store, at least not at these rents. But the kiosk is a perfect venue. This is another way that suburbia gets multicultural—most of the mall's shoppers will never even see one of these miniature tuxedos (complete with bow tie and waistcoat) that some Hispanic babies will wear to the baptismal font unless they see them here.

Most often, however, the pushcart world is populated with sunglasses, cell phones, costume jewelry, and the "As Seen on TV" shop. At first the malls thought the kiosks would be like an incubator—that today's pushcart would grow into tomorrow's store tenant. But that hasn't been the case. More common is the kiosk entrepreneur who expands numerically, growing from one cart to several (in separate malls) to many.

On a Saturday afternoon you may have thirty-three hundred people an hour passing a kiosk in a good spot. In our research we've found that more than half of the people in a mall will at least look at a pushcart and maybe 6 percent will actually shop one. They're especially popular among women twenty-five to thirty-four, who are most avidly seeking out the novel and the new.

Kiosks aren't the only things sticking out in the middle of the mall.

Car dealers are fond of sticking their new models in mall thoroughfares. It's a good idea, especially because there's precious little intended for men and boys here as it is. You can easily kill a few minutes checking out the latest Mini or Maserati. I don't know that a Saturn or Subaru or anything else that's already abundant in suburbia would make as much sense. And since women now either buy or influence the purchase of half of all cars sold in this country, the dealers are wise to reach them here in the mall. It's a great way to experience a car up close without having to talk to a car salesman or enter a dealership, which is an automatic plus in my book.

We're coming up on something now that's a cross between a kiosk and a resting place—a display of massaging easy chairs set right out in the main thoroughfare. You become part of the display the second you sit, which doesn't seem to bother those shoppers who are in the mood for an electric rubdown.

"Hey, how's it going?" I greet the chair's minder as I sit.

"Hi," the Asian man responds.

You see these chairs everywhere in Japan—they sell them in electronics stores. Usually they're set up in front of the TVs, so you can watch and try the chair, allowing you to sample it in a naturalistic setting.

"What's the wattage to run this chair?" I ask.

"Two-ten watts."

"Two lightbulbs."

"Yes. Like TV or refrigerator."

"Okay, and is this the price, $3,500?"

Not cheap by a long shot. A lot more than you'd expect to pay for a piece of furniture that's being sold right off the mall floor, without even a store to lend it an air of authority.

"Yes, plus shipping."

"Where is it made?"

"In Japan."

This display will be here for maybe a month, tops, and then they'll move on to another mall. It will get the most attention and trial use on the weekend, but I bet they don't sell a single chair from Friday to Sunday. These are commonplace in Asian homes, and they sell here mostly to Asian families. And there are now a lot of Koreans and Chinese and Taiwanese around here, as there are in and around most big cities. The serious buyers will come in during the week, when the mall is quieter, and buy then. For us curious browsers, it's a nice little stop.

Nice unless you're working inside the fancy healthy-back furniture store, I mean, where they also sell expensive electronic massage chairs.

"Come on, try the chair!" the saleslady coaxes when she notices me eyeing it. "What are you waiting for?"

"Have you seen the massage chairs out there in the mall?" I ask as I take a seat.

"Well, they're two different things," she says, smiling a little less. "What we sell here and what they sell there. We try to emphasize . . . that chair is too small for you."

She's referring to my height, in case you leapt to some erroneous conclusion.

"To answer your question," she says, "the same people who check out their chairs then come in here to compare them with what we have."

"And . . . ?"

"And so far we've had quite good responses to our chairs. You can adjust ours. You can select the spots you want massaged. In their chair, the spots are already set up. And we have two models. The one you're in is pretty much the same as theirs. It sells for $3,500."

"Same as theirs."

"Yes. But our *other* model sells for just $1,800. And the parts for our chairs are made by the same company that makes theirs. It's a little bit bad for us that they're allowed to be in our part of the mall, because they can be out there in the mall itself, and they can have more than one chair. But our store puts more of an emphasis on the ergonomics."

"Right."

"And on your back."

"Like with that $8,000 mattress?"

"Yes! Have you tried it yet?"

So far as I know, there's no mall that allows shoppers to try mattresses out in the main thoroughfare. So while the kiosks have their place, there's still something to be said for a store.

14 Mall Cuisine

I'M HUNGRY.

Personally, I am no fan of the mall's signature dining experience—the food court. I find them painfully noisy. Food courts are all hard surfaces, which are both durable and easy to clean. Tile, linoleum, Formica, stainless steel, and glass are all practical materials, except they turn the typically cavernous space into a giant echo chamber. The clamor of hungry shoppers creates quite a din. It's interesting to note that many of the most stylish restaurants and bars in Manhattan have this trait in common with the humble mall food court.

The noise makes it impossible for me to discern normal conversation. This means I'd normally stay far away from the food court, except as a place to study an important part of mall life. Feeding time.

We need food at the mall because, it seems, we need food everywhere. It's hard to think of a public space in America that doesn't offer up at least a few opportunities to eat. Each has its signature dish, too—

hot dogs at the ballpark (along with peanuts and Cracker Jack), pop-corn at the movies, and any number of delicacies on city streets. (I'm a traditionalist, and so I wait eagerly for roasted chestnut season on the streets of New York.) At the mall, you've usually got your pick of freshly baked chocolate chip cookie outlets, and by now we associate the pow-erful, Proustian aroma of Cinnabon with indoor shopping.

But the food court is the big act. Forget for a moment the quality of the food itself and focus on how it assembles dishes from every corner of the planet. Is there another place where the quasi-foodstuffs of Mexico, China, Italy, Thailand, Greece, Japan, and South Philadelphia come together like this?

From the mall's perspective, the food court has an important role—to prolong the shopper's stay. Without some kind of food you're good for two, maybe three hours before exhaustion overtakes you and sends you running for sustenance. Thanks to the food court, you can shop to the verge of starvation, fuel up, and maybe get in another hour or two. There's nothing inherently brilliant about food courts—the street ven-dors of hot dogs and ice cream and pretzels found in most downtowns serve the same function of feeding you quickly while holding you within the grasp of retail's visual come-ons. Depending on which city you're in, urban street eats are probably more adventurous than what you'll find at the chains, which predominate the food courts. Within two blocks of my office I can grab (depending on the time of year) some street vendor shish kebob, souvlakia, curry, hot dogs, a cross sec-tion of gourmet sausages, soft pretzels, sugar-coated nuts or coconut, bagels, falafel, knishes, Italian ices, pizza or calzones (from a pizzeria with a street side window).

Is food court food any good? It's good enough, I guess. If I were a suburban fifteen-year-old who had never experienced any delicacy more subtle than a Double Whopper, I wouldn't sneer at what I found here or wish for the barbequed eel roll from my favorite sushi joint. Nobody goes to the mall expecting anything more than a plastic tray full of edible nourishment and a clean table on which to enjoy it. Who are we to sneer?

The food court serves as the mall's Via Veneto, its main concourse for sitting and supping and sipping and people watching. I keep hoping

to find one that takes this responsibility seriously—an ambitious food
court that imagines itself as a huge sidewalk café, where tables all have
a view not just of one another (clearly taken from the court's fast-food
restaurant ancestry) but of the mall's main thoroughfares, with tables
even spilling out a little into the corridors. I haven't found one yet.

The typical per person food court expenditure comes to around $6
or so, making it hard to complain too loudly. In fact, you'd find yourself
hard-pressed to spend much more than that, which could be seen as a
shortcoming of the operation. There may be shoppers willing to spend
twice that $6 figure in the food court, but nobody to my knowledge has
begun to find out. Where's the food court wine bar? The French
bistro? If somebody knows, please send up a flare.

Let's move on and find one of the sit-down restaurants, which, luckily, this mall has in sufficient supply. Usually you'll find at least one or
two, depending on the overall tenor of the mall. They're usually chains,
which nowadays doesn't necessarily mean the food will be bland and
inferior and the service awkward but chipper. Of course, neither are
most mall restaurants the site of memorable dining. Wolfgang Puck has
a few boîtes in malls, but by and large we end up with generic chain-
restaurant fare.

In Japan, by way of contrast, restaurants and prepared-food shops at
malls are of such high quality that many people stop there daily, on the
way home, to pick up dinner. In any city there are plenty of good
restaurants and takeout places that serve that purpose. Suburbanites,
however, find limited choices in the prepared-foods department. Pizza,
fast food, maybe a Boston Chicken, and whatever the local supermarket dishes up, and that's about it. If you're lucky you live near an ambitious diner, or a locally owned restaurant that takes itself seriously (and
does takeout). In New York, there's a grocer/prepared-food shop in
Grand Central Station that's always jammed at evening rush hour with
suburban commuters picking up that night's dinner. If American malls'
food operations took themselves more seriously as providers of meals,
some of those people would no doubt grab something closer to home.

Interestingly, in one big mall we studied, one out of four people in
the common area (*not* in the food court or a restaurant) were eating
something. Some of these were having coffee or a chocolate chip

cookie while walking, sitting on a bench, or leaning against a wall. Some had brought snacks from home. So it's clear that even food courts aren't capacious enough to house all the eating that goes on in a mall. Also, some food bought in the court migrates into the corridors of the mall itself. That, no doubt, is how some people express their dislike of the food court—they eat on the hoof, or while perched on the edge of the fountain. Given how often and how much we Americans eat, we must be willing to do it pretty much anywhere and everywhere, and certainly the mall lends itself to that—the surfaces are easy to clean, and everybody else is eating anyway.

At two points in my twenties I asked women to marry me. I got turned down on both occasions. Those two low points in my life were handed to me by ladies from Louisiana. More times than I'd like to admit, I wander into the Cajun joint in a mall food court, indulge in some Bourbon Chicken and Dirty Rice, and daydream over what might have been. Today is no exception.

15 *Breakfast at Cartier*

"OKAY," I SAY, "pay attention to that woman window shopping."

We're standing at an interesting spot in the mall, able to see both Cartier, the ultra-luxury French jewerly retailer, and its next-door neighbor, a discount jewelry chain.

"What's she going to do?"

"Hard to say. That's why we're paying attention."

I'm with Albert, a normal middle-aged guy, meaning there are a dozen places he'd rather be right now than here. He's shopping for jewelry for his wife. We've already scanned the Cartier window, which at this moment has that lady shopper's attention, and so we know it contains what's called a tennis bracelet—so named because Chris Evert, at the 1987 U.S. Open, dropped a diamond bracelet during a match and stopped play until she found it—a costly bauble in which a dozen or so round diamonds have been set in a straight row.

This is an interesting juxtaposition of stores, one engineered by the mall leasing office, which closely controls who goes where. The thinking is that if you create a little cluster of stores that will attract like-minded shoppers, you increase sales for everybody (especially for the mall itself, which takes a piece of every dollar spent). It allows today's time-pressed shopper to hit one part of a mall, visit several stores that carry what he or she has in mind, and get the job done efficiently. But it's certainly not a new-fangled idea—for centuries at least, stores have organized into districts based on what they sell.

Jewelry especially lends itself to districts. Since buying it isn't an everyday experience, there's a degree of comfort in being able to shop more than one store. It also has historic roots. For example, however different in character, London has Old Bond Street, New York City has Forty-seventh Street, Istanbul has its Grand Bazaar, where jewelry dealers congregate. Another purchase that historically has gained synergy from concentration is the art gallery. All are designed to help the underexperienced gain the courage to say "I'll take it." There is another reason, too.

At the mall, clustering by category gives the shopper a chance to make the circuit. In some cases, the stores are clustered into a good-better-best arrangement, though for the novice buyer it may be hard to discern the difference. That good-better-best setup usually involves a degree of overlap in prices and products. In some cases, the same company may own more than one of the stores in the cluster.

Back in my urban-planner life, we studied pedestrian traffic along Forty-second Street in Manhattan in the "bad old days" of Times Square. Many New Yorkers cheered when former mayor Rudolph W. Giuliani rid the district of its pornographic sleaze and overall decay and Disney-fied it for family consumption. The fetid live peepshows were replaced by *The Lion King* and Madame Tussaud's Wax Museum, making the area safe for tourists, who now flock there to enjoy a dazzling variety of wholesome fare. It really was an ugly, seamy part of town back then, and yet there was something admirably authentic about it— it was one district among many in this city, a kind of partitioning that gave New York a great deal of its flavor. The porn zone served a purpose, and just because it's moved doesn't mean we're all nicer creatures where sex is concerned.

We urban-planner types would stand on the roofs of buildings and watch how pedestrians made their way down the street. We saw countless male strollers approach the strip of porn shops. Typically, they'd reach the first one and slow down a little. You could tell by that and how they'd turn their heads that the storefronts had gotten their attention. But they almost never entered the first store they reached. They'd gradually cruise to a stop by the second or third shop on the block, and that's the one they'd enter (after doing a quick head swivel to make sure no office colleagues were watching).

That's the effect of clustering on retailers. Shoppers who are intent on visiting a particular store will find it without any help. But the cluster slows the walking speed of the casual pedestrian, the one who may have had no intention of stopping. The first store causes you to hit the brakes, and by the second or third you've slowed down enough to pay attention. Once inside a store you may fail to find exactly what you want, but then you're close to other shops offering the same kind of goods, and, before you know it, you're shopping. That's one way in which the dynamic of the mall serves both the business and the customer at the same time.

In this particular cluster we've got Cartier, and just down the corridor a little way there's Tiffany & Co., and across from that there's Ralph Lauren, and one or two other high-end shops, too. It's a mini-mall here of fancy stores, something to make life a little more convenient for the shopper with money to spend.

What scares the Cartiers and Tiffanys of the world is the number of people who will walk past their stores without ever thinking about stopping. That's why these swanky retailers find themselves in the improbable setting of the mall. The flagship stores retain all the cachet of their fancy Fifth Avenue locations. But the business has to go where the shoppers are, and that means suburbia, especially affluent suburbs such as the ones that ring this mall. How often does the average suburban shopper make her or his way into town for the total Tiffany experience? Can you blame them? You're talking about devoting most of a day to such a venture. Who has that kind of time?

Albert's office isn't so far from the Tiffany store on Fifth Avenue, but he's busy working all day, and lunch hour ends up being the most crowded time. So even being two blocks away from *the* Tiffany's, a worldwide landmark, doesn't make it easier to shop the store. Whereas on a Saturday like today, without Christmas or Valentine's Day looming, the mall store is tranquil. And so what if Cartier and Tiffany have to go a little mass-market and mingle with the hoi polloi? They'll find a way to exist more or less at ease in the mall, even right next door to a discount jeweler.

It's interesting to see how the translation of luxury to the mall plays out. The issues begin at the lease line with decisions about the stores' facades. Everywhere else in the mall, as we've seen, design decisions make access to the stores as effortless as possible—yawning entrances, lots of plate glass, as little facade as possible, in keeping with the ideals of transparency and lack of pretense or anything else that might discourage a shopper from entering.

Here, however, you've got some competing values. The last thing Cartier wants is to seem as approachable and affordable as, say, the Gap. No matter where it exists, Cartier has to uphold its defining values, and a significant part of that is how it looks. There's something about fancy jewelry that requires an air of exclusivity, solidity—it wants to evoke a bit of the fortress in its very choice of home. Again, stroll Fifth Avenue and see how Harry Winston, Bvlgari, Tiffany, and Cartier do it up. How then do you say Cartier in the vocabulary of a mall?

You start by defying the mall's characteristic transparency, judging by how these stores do it. The equation seems sensible enough: the cheaper the goods, the more visible they are. Or, the more precious the merchandise, the less glass to show it off. Someone decided to clad the entire facade of the store in a black stone that appears to be slate. It makes a statement in the context of the mall—no other store comes close to creating such a definite distinction between *out there* and *in here.* The windows are small squares of light set in those black walls, which succeeds in focusing the passing shoppers' gaze. It *feels* expensive.

"So that's the question," I tell Albert. "How does Cartier dress for the suburbs?"

"How about a really nice track suit?" he says.

"Well, it needs to do something along those lines. It has to say

Cartier. But it has to do so in a way that is appropriate to the setting. It can't feel exactly like Fifth Avenue. There, a store can be understated in its presentation. There are enough other signals reaching the passerby. You know it's a high-end store, whereas here even Cartier needs to tell its story."

"Do the black walls say it?"

"I'm not sure. Do they seem a little forbidding?"

"Isn't that the point?"

"Well, to some degree, yes. They don't want every passerby to think he or she belongs inside the store."

"That's an unusual message for a store, isn't it? 'Dear shopper, stay out!' "

"Not really. Every store has to deliver that message. Just that some stores want lots of people inside, and other ones—like this one—don't. Cartier would suffer if tomorrow every hayseed walking down the mall corridor got the impression that he was welcome inside. Cartier's genuine customers wouldn't stand for it."

Our company has done studies for Bvlgari, the exclusive Italian jeweler. At their stores, they informed me, they don't want good visibility from outside to inside. They say it's because if Mrs. Rossi walks by and sees Mr. Bianco inside, buying something costly, she might go to Mrs. Bianco and say, "Oh, I saw your husband in Bvlgari the other day buying you a beautiful emerald necklace," and then Mrs. Bianco waits and waits for the gift before realizing that it must have gone to another woman. Maybe that's more of a concern in Europe than it is here. But it becomes part of the store's culture, that discretion, that sophistication. Even for shoppers in the Americas or Asia, it helps impart that European flavor. That's why at most jewelers, the really expensive diamonds and so on are kept in a small, secluded room in the very rear of the store.

"I thought that was so nobody would steal them," Albert says.

He's right, in part—a jewelry store puts the costliest goods at some distance from the front door for security reasons. But thieves still get away with the old grab and run. We did a research job for a luxury jeweler in L.A., and one problem with the store was its lousy lighting. The designer clearly had never spent much time around jewelry, and as a result shoppers wanted to bring merchandise close to the front windows, so they could see it in natural light. But the store got stung a couple times. The jewelry kept going all the way out the door.

Just last year, at a fancy store in New York, something like that happened when a well-dressed man asked to see a ruby and diamond ring. The clerk handed it over, and the customer turned to face the window, to see it in daylight. At that moment a young woman entered the store, at which point the man tossed her the ring. She caught it like a major leaguer and dashed back outside into a waiting car, which sped away. It happened so fast that all the security guard could do was watch. And as he watched the man just melted away. A smart little caper.

"I like it," Albert says. "Has somebody ever tried it in a mall?"

"How would you make your escape from up here on the second level to your getaway car?"

"And then what if you forget where you parked?"

This is one reason retailers like malls over streets—security is a breeze in here compared to out there. Yet, jewelry store symbolism remains the same in either locale. You sell the really good gems way in back. It's like the innermost sanctum—the vault, as it were. You shouldn't be able to see the best diamonds from outside the store, otherwise where's the mystery and drama? In this fashion, store design functions as a narrative device, drawing you deeper into the story. But that kind of thinking is totally contrary to how most mall stores operate. This is an issue because this store has to make itself accessible to other stores' shoppers. That's the whole point of being in a mall. Malls put somebody else's customers in your store.

Of course, city streets do the same thing. And yet, it's different. On Fifth Avenue, for instance, there are many pedestrians walking by the store on any given day, many more than in this mall. Even though most of those people don't go into Cartier. In fact, a great many of the people walking Fifth Avenue aren't even on shopping trips. They work in the area, or they're on their way to a hotel or a restaurant or to the park. But Cartier's customers know where to find the store. And Fifth Avenue itself draws people from around the world who know it as one of the planet's premiere shopping districts.

As a result, there will be Tiffany customers, or Gucci customers, who will make their way to Cartier. But this corridor is not Fifth Avenue, and, from where I'm standing, I can see the sneaker store and the store that specializes in overpriced, trendy T-shirts for teenage girls, and the dress shop for overweight women buying midpriced frocks. The Cartier name doesn't usually find itself in such company. And so it needs to figure out how to attract shoppers—certain shoppers—while discouraging others. It needs to take advantage of being in a mall that draws large numbers of people without the means to buy anything in Cartier, or even any intention of entering a luxury goods store with a haughty reputation.

So Cartier and stores like it must somehow select the shoppers who will walk in the door. There are three categories of people in this mall, at least where this store is concerned. One group is Cartier customers. Another is people who could be Cartier customers, but haven't ever gone inside. And the third is people who will never be customers. The store needs to attract everybody in category one. That seems easy enough, but that's the smallest category. It also wants to get some from category two. Finally, it wants to attract the attention of those in the third group, give them a bit of an education, but make sure they just look at the windows and are too intimidated to pass over the threshold. The store wants to pick certain people out of the crowd. It wants to send a message—"You, yes, and you, but not you."

The store must take care not to undercut that ambience with shoddy materials or workmanship, even around the edge of a facade in a mall that's thousands of miles away from Paris. After all, the most expensive piece in the whole place is probably smaller than a nickel. People who come in here have their eyes focused on tiny items—the scale by the very nature of the merchandise is small. You can't tell shoppers to examine this little diamond but ignore that smudged window, or the gray plastic trash can in the corner.

"Hey, where's the lady who was looking at the tennis bracelet?"

"She bounced off the Cartier storefront and went into the discount jeweler next door."

The relationship between Cartier and the discount joint next door is intriguing. It's easy to see how the cut-rate neighbor benefits from having such luxury so close at hand. Your appetite is whetted by Cartier's window. You covet what's in there. But you can't afford it, most likely. So you go next door, which you *can* afford, and buy there.

"How could it help the fancy store?" Albert asks.

"Well, once in a while, it might. Maybe you'll walk out of the discount place thinking it's beneath you, you'll feel brave enough to see what life is like in the big leagues. Or maybe a window-shopping couple will check out the discounter first, and then one will gently lead the other to the fine jeweler."

"But isn't the discounter likely to reap more benefits from being next to Cartier?"

"Possibly. That's partly because Cartier is not meant to capture a high percentage of the people walking this mall. But it also has a lot to do with the changing nature of jewelry purchases. Traditionally, jewelry has been purchased by men for women, in three basic arrangements. The first is as keys to the front door—call it engagement, anniversary, birthday—all public statements of affection and intention. The second is keys to the back door, which are presents to mistresses or girlfriends that are meant to ensure access, but bypass all the front-door commitments. The third category, which for the jeweler has traditionally been important, is the keys out of the doghouse, or the purchases meant to make amends for bad behavior. Flowers are nice, but of limited power to affect a woman's mind. Nothing says 'Dear, I am *so* sorry!' like a gold necklace or a pair of diamond earrings." I let that sink in before asking, "Albert, are you going for the front door or are you trying to get out of the doghouse?"

"Front, I guess," he says. "It's her birthday soon."

"I see. Why jewelry?"

"For Christmas I got her an extremely high-quality radio that she said she wanted."

"Did she appreciate it?"

"I think so. But I got the impression that I shouldn't get anything that plugs in for her birthday gift. It is in the same family of moves as giving your mother a new catcher's mitt."

Jewelry stores are not keeping up with social change. For instance, in 1993 a study of gold jewelry buying habits found that for the first time ever, women were buying more of it for themselves than men were buying for them. While the key and door thing are still a big part of the business, an important piece of the business has changed forever.

That change requires a new way of thinking about jewelry and selling it, too. All of a sudden, jewelers have to sell two ways from one store. In order to do that, they've got to rethink the premises, which not a lot of stores are doing well, even though this shift is more than a decade old. Jewelry is now closer than ever to fine fashion, at least when women buy it. As with apparel, women are more conscious about how they appear to one another than how they look to men. When a man looks at models in couture, he looks at the woman more than the outfit. Similarly, he's not looking at a necklace or a bracelet the way a woman does—he's not registering the details or the overall effect the same way she does. He's not considering how it will feel to wear it. She most certainly is. Jewelers haven't yet caught up with that distinction.

For instance, most jewelry stores do mirrors badly. There aren't enough of them. And they tend to be awkwardly placed—either on top of counters that aren't near the jewelry cases, or hanging on the walls. Again, the assumption is that the person buying the jewelry isn't the one who will wear it. A shopper is faced with expensive display cases and black velvet swags and high-powered ceiling spotlights that make every diamond sparkle like Liz Taylor's fist. And mediocre mirrors. The assumption is that the mirror scheme doesn't have to perform the same function as it does in, say, Armani. Even cosmetics departments do mirrors better than jewelers do.

This should be easy enough to fix, but the problem doesn't stop there.

The entire jewelry store traditionally plays to a certain fantasy—the one of the guy who's rich and powerful enough to afford something for the woman who's beautiful and desirable enough, with exquisite taste in adornment, to deserve what's here. Once women start buying their own baubles, however, the store needs to accommodate a second fantasy. This one is about dress-up, a game most women have been playing in one form or another since childhood. It's also about self-reward, and making the leap between who she is and who she wants to be.

But it also has to do with the professional woman who is making good money and has been around enough to know what Cartier quality means. She believes she deserves it, and has no problem with buying it for herself, just as she buys Donna Karan or Dolce&Gabbana. She may have a rich husband. She may have *no* husband. She may be married to a man who earns less than she does—in fact, maybe while she's in the store she'll also shop for *him*. The jewelry store now has to create the fantasy that comes with how women adorn themselves, the way Armani or Versace sell their goods to women. Go to those stores and see what the entire trying-on experience is like. It's aimed at the wearer. It assumes she's the decision maker. The dressing room is expensively decorated and immaculate. The mirrors are large and properly placed. The lights are flattering and may even show how she'll look under a variety of kinds of illumination. The sales help is attentive and respectful. A woman tries on an Armani suit or a Versace evening gown and she feels like a movie star. She gets a taste of how the rest of the world is going to see her and respond if she buys that garment. That's what a jeweler now must attempt to do.

There's also another strategy for selling jewelry to that woman, way down at the other end of the spectrum. Because if a woman is shopping for herself, maybe she doesn't need *any* romance or fantasy with her jewelry. We're not yet at the point where diamond earrings in a vending machine will work. But it's interesting to note that Wal-Mart and Sam's Club are now major jewelry retailers, and not just inexpensive goods—even big-ticket diamonds, pearls, and watches. Once upon a time, the person who was likely to buy expensive jewelry would never have shopped at a discount store or buying club for *anything*. But those days are gone. This has been one of the most significant changes in shopping patterns of the past quarter century—that people now go to Neiman Marcus in the morning and Wal-Mart in the afternoon. The walls have all come down, and today there's a lot less shopper snobbery that used to keep all the luxury retailers so contented. Women especially will buy for less if they can. And while Armani is available only at the pricier stores, diamonds and gold and emeralds and pearls can be found anywhere. The woman who decides to buy herself a pair of good diamond stud earrings might as well go to a discounter—after all, she doesn't need to impress or seduce herself.

"So instead of going into Cartier," I say, "let's go visit the discounter next door."

"Is that big 50% OFF SALE! sign in the window a good idea?"

"Probably. You don't see Cartier yelling sale, do you?"

"Hey, how you doing?" That's the manager of the discount jeweler talking. We're in his store now. It's a perfectly nice place to buy jewelry. There are no dark woods or heavy-duty facade to reinforce the feeling that you've entered a magic zone. In fact, there are no exterior walls at all—you just kind of veer in from the mall corridor—and all the display cases are glass with metal or pale wood. The decor is kind of feminine-neutral, with pinkish accents here and there. And the clerk—there's just one—is an affable guy in a plaid sports jacket and red tie.

"We're fine! How 'bout you?"

"Fine!"

"Hey, how often do you have to clean your glass here?" I ask, pointing to the big display case up front.

"Well, let me put it this way—if I had a penny for every time I've done it, I could retire right now. I use a lot of Windex. It gets dirty fast."

Another difference between here and next door is the layout. At Cartier there's a definite barrier between the shopper and the salesperson. The display cases act as a barricade, practically—they're there to hold and show the goods, but they also tell you, the customer, to keep your distance. That design decision is old-school—all stores once operated that way, but today it's fading fast. That layout set the tone for the transaction: it became a face-to-face, head-to-head thing, like the offense and defense lined up against each other on a football field. You, the shopper, had the money, and it was the salesclerk's job to get it from you. Certainly the tone was never overtly adversarial, but the undertone, I think, was just that.

Then, that cosmetics innovation known as the "open sell" became the rage in jewelry retailing, too. In this configuration, all the goods are out in front of the counter where the shopper can touch and try them on, unaided. In so many stores nowadays there are none of the long, low counters that once filled every shop. Even in this jewelry store, the clerk no longer hides behind the counter. He's right next to you, helping you try on the necklace, and looking into the mirror with you.

"You know, I like how the display cases are set up."

"Yep—me, too," he says. "It doesn't help to be standing behind a counter. It used to be that way right here—counter, counter, counter. But when they remodeled it, they took the counters away."

"How much of your business comes in here after being in Cartier first?"

"A lot do, actually. See this necklace here? They sell one like it for many thousands of dollars, solid gold. Ours is costume, but it sells for $139, and, believe me, you can't tell them apart. So most people, if they can save some money and nobody's ever going to notice anyway, they'll do it. Of course, then there are people who have hundreds of thousands to spend on jewelry, and who am I to argue with them?"

"So you stock this store partly in response to what they're selling at Cartier and Tiffany?"

"Yes, indeed. I don't know if my bosses chose this location because it's next to Cartier and down the hall from Tiffany, but it helps. See this choker? You can go to Tiffany and get it for $81,000, that's no lie, or you can get it here for $349. And nobody's going to know whether they're real pearls or not unless they come over and begin gnawing on your necklace!"

"Do you think that ever happens?"

"Not to me it doesn't!"

Albert and I amble a few stores down, to Tiffany. The first thing we see in the window is something the store doesn't even sell—a beautiful black and white photograph of what could be either Paris or maybe Central Park, in the rain. The other most prominent thing here is the Tiffany logo.

"This window isn't selling jewelry, necessarily—it's selling Tiffany," I observe.

"That's a good idea, right?"

"Well, anything's a good idea if it works. I would say it works on some levels really well. The fact is that while Tiffany and Cartier are both world-class names in luxury goods, Tiffany is better known in the U.S."

"There's no Breakfast at Cartier, is there?"

"Not yet. Somehow, Audrey Hepburn and Tiffany became synonymous. She's now their dead celebrity spokesperson."

How this window display works in the mall, though, is an entirely different matter. Here, it seems intended to evoke the Manhattan flagship store and make the connection for the out-of-town mall shopper, especially tourists from abroad. That in itself is remarkable, because, typically, malls don't do much to accommodate foreign shoppers. That's probably because Americans don't think that way. We just don't feel dependent on international trade, even though we really are. Because this mall is near a major metropolitan area, however, the surrounding suburbs are home to many foreigners here either permanently or while working in the states. Lots of Asians—Indians, Koreans, Chinese, Japanese. Lots of Middle Easterners, too, all of whom are familiar with the Tiffany name and reputation. So it makes huge sense to work the brand.

Also, Tiffany is famous for its windows. The Manhattan store puts a great deal of money and effort into them, although they are minuscule by the standards of department store windows. In New York, the windows that get most local buzz around the holidays are Tiffany's and Barney's. The big, glitzy, droll displays at Barney's have become as much a signature as Tiffany's beautiful, elegant, gemlike windows. This window treatment here in the mall is different from what is done in the city. It sells the romance of Central Park in the rain, and being very near to Tiffany, to people who are walking around a mall. That's a good goal.

"Even though the window doesn't have a single piece of jewelry in it?" Albert asks.

"I guess you could buy that silver picture frame in the window. And Tiffany is known for its silver, too. This is Tiffany's being discreet."

"Does all that mean Tiffany will do better in this mall than Cartier?"

"I think that depends on what happens inside. As in most malls, the jewelry stores here are all clustered, so even if you do find something you like in Tiffany, it's very easy to take two minutes to make sure you can't find the same thing a little nicer, or a little cheaper, at Cartier. And this window is very good but not exactly perfect either."

"What's wrong with it?"

"Well, Tiffany is selling New York, that's for sure, and people are fond of New York these days. But Tiffany also is selling a color and a bag. That particular shade of blue, on a shopping bag, announces *Tiffany* even before you see the logo. It's maybe the most successful shopping bag ever. But there's no blue and no bag in the window. Forget the bag—there's not a trace of the blue."

That brings us back to our question of why this merchandise is in the window. The answer seems clear: Because it appeals to women. The windows in the city store play to the fantasy wherein the man gives the bauble to the woman. Here in the mall, perhaps wisely, the window plays to her alone. As we said before, perhaps it's her money, and she wants silver. Or maybe the kids are out of college, and her husband just bought himself that Mercedes two-seater convertible. Now it's her turn for a treat. Either way, more than ever before, it's the woman making the big-ticket luxury purchase. And jewelers have to adapt.

"Hey," Albert says, "there's a smudge on the window."

"You know, the French have an expression for window shopping: They say, *Il faut que je lèche les vitrines.'* Meaning, 'I need to go lick the windows.' And window displays there are often called *lèche-vitrines.*"

"What do you think of this door?"

"Steely," I say. "Sturdy. A real urban doorway. A clear line between out there in the mall and in here at Tiffany's, and there's no accidental crossing between one and the other."

"Not friendly in the mall way, is it?"

"No. Not actually unfriendly, either. Warm, natural shades. The metal is stainless steel, or looks that way, which is kind of stylish these days. But maybe it's a little clumsy."

"How is this different from the store on Fifth Avenue?"

"It's not so different, but here in the mall people have come to expect that they can cross in and out of stores effortlessly. A big, heavy door feels weird. It feels wrong. At the Cartier store there was a doorman, a friendly guy in a handsome suit who would smile at you if you even came close to the door, and he'd open it grandly for you, as though he was certain you meant to spend a lot of dough inside."

"No doorman here."

"Right. Look inside, though, and you'll see the security guard. That's probably the same function Cartier's doorman served, except he also made it easier to get into the place. That was a very smart decision by somebody. Jewelers need a security presence at the doorway, so why not have him also open the damn thing?"

"Have you gentlemen seen anything yet?"

"No, thanks."

"Well, let me know if you do."

"Thanks."

"The other problem for Tiffany and Cartier and every other jeweler," I explain to Albert but also to the saleswoman, who is hovering, "is the changing nature of our relationship to adornment. We have so many ways of adorning ourselves, and of telling the world who we are. Jewelry once was universally accepted as a way of announcing one's wealth and position. It's an ancient means for expressing all that, and continues to hold that place among many of the world's cultures."

Consider the dot-com millionaires—they have (or had) plenty of money, but they didn't spend it on the same things that earlier generations of tycoons did. The younger moguls seemed not as comfortable with the conspicuous adornment of gems and precious metals. They were okay buying houses. Cars. Eminently capable of choosing ostentatious kitchen appliances—Viking stoves and Sub-Zero refrigerators. Home spas. Porsche now sells an SUV, joining Mercedes, Lexus, and Cadillac. That's the status symbol of our era—on the one hand it's a truck, totally lacking in glamour, suitable for hauling kids or lawn-care products. And yet it costs a fortune to own and another fortune to gas it up. It's the status symbol for people who scorn status symbols.

The New Age tycoon may spend $1,000 on a bottle of wine or $8,000 on a laptop computer or $200,000 for an oceanfront rental in Southampton. But he won't drop $50,000 for a piece of jewelry, even one of the highest quality, which could be handed down for generations. He doesn't feel comfortable walking into a jewelry store and plunking down that kind of cash for something that is essentially decorative.

And, once again, we must consider the changing status of women within the lives of men. She used to be comfortable with her role as a mannequin on which he would hang symbols of wealth, power, and taste. You could look at a woman and learn a great deal about her man. Certainly, he wasn't wearing any obvious adornments—that was *her* job.

"Let me ask you something," Albert says. "That dot-com tycoon, is it that he doesn't buy jewelry, or that he doesn't like the idea of buying it in this old-fashioned big-spender kind of store?"

"It's funny you say that," I tell him. "Because the only diamond I've ever bought in my life, I bought at a Sam's Club."

"The place where people go to buy toilet paper in bulk? Now, did you go to the store thinking, 'Gee, today I need to buy a diamond necklace, where should I go?' "

"You know, somebody who's an expert in these matters mentioned to me that if you want to get the most for your money, buy jewelry at Sam's Club. That the jewelry is of the same quality as you find in a jewelry store, but the price is quite a bit lower."

"Did the box say 'Sam's Club' on it?"

"No, actually I didn't care for the box it came in, so I bought another one, something nicer."

"Does your beloved know you got it at Sam's?"

"She will when she reads this. The next year I did get her something at Tiffany. But my point is that this is how people shop today. Not every man needs to feel like the big spender who goes into Tiffany or Cartier or Bvlgari and drops a fortune on gems for his lady. Time has passed that paradigm by, and jewelry stores still haven't figured out what to try next."

"What was the experience like, buying expensive diamond jewelry in a buyer's club with all the crates of cornflakes on palettes?"

"I just told the clerk here's what I want, and she showed me three different versions and I bought the most expensive."

"Were you trying to get in the front door or the back door?"

"It was a Christmas present."

One way the relations between the sexes have changed is that men—especially younger men—often don't have to work as hard as they used to to get in either door. Or maybe today relationships are over quicker. Perhaps if he senses that this woman isn't a lifelong mate, maybe it's better to spend the money on a vacation, something he can enjoy, too, rather than watch her walk out the door wearing the $10,000 Rolex watch he gave her. I mean, how many marriages even make it to the tenth anniversary?

"Or what if she says, 'But honey, what I really wanted was something practical, like a radio?' " Albert says.

"One of the most poignant retail stories I ever heard was from the jewelry business. A jeweler I know described how this middle-aged man came into his shop one day. The guy explained that he was a mechanic, and had a bunch of kids, and so was never able to afford a proper ring for his wife. Now it was their twentieth anniversary coming up, and he had managed to set aside a few bucks to buy something nice. And with that he reached into his jeans pocket and pulled out these crumpled bills, like $250 or so. It was a fairly small sum for this particular store, but the jeweler described to me the pleasure he felt in taking this working man and helping him find a really nice ring, with a tiny diamond in it, for his wife. I mean, that's the kind of moment that happens in a jewelry store. You'll never get that kind of emotional pay-off selling jeans or sneakers or video games. But jewelers haven't figured out how to capitalize on that old-fashioned thing while feeling contemporary, too."

"How might they sell that mechanic's moment?"

"Any number of ways. Maybe a little lifestyle graphic right—"

"What do you mean by 'lifestyle'?"

This was from the Tiffany salesperson.

"Well, like a photo or something . . ." I reply. That's when she notices that I have a small tape recorder along for the ride.

"We're being recorded?" she asks, suddenly suspicious.

"Hey, nice wall," I say, pointing to a large display of Tiffany boxes.

This is an evasive maneuver, but what I'm pointing to is actually a good idea, something I'd noticed before. It takes fullest advantage of the signature blue box: Small, modestly priced gifts, such as silver keychains or money clips, already boxed and ready to go. It provides a huge visual hit of that Tiffany blue, something the store needs. It is designed for gifts a bride gives to her wedding party. The hope is that the customer buys eight, not one. It also offers something affordable to the hesitant shopper who entered thinking there's no way he'd find some-thing in here, while (because it's preboxed) not requiring much sales-clerk attention. It is the jewelry store version of the cosmetics "open sell."

"We're being recorded?" she persists, now on full red alert. "Be-cause you can't . . . I didn't realize you had . . ."

"I'm not recording you," I say. "I'm recording me."

"Well, I don't want anything that I said—"

"Neither do I," says a second clerk, who hasn't even been close until now.

"Because we'll be in big trouble," says the first clerk, "because we're not supposed to record or have pictures taken—"

❋　❋　❋

We had seen enough of the store, and we're now back in the safety of the mall proper. Albert still hasn't gotten his wife a gift—in truth, he has barely looked at the goods—but each shopper has a unique style, like a DNA fingerprint. Something tells me his style incorporates a great deal of procrastination, followed by a panicky trip (maybe back to this same mall) at the eleventh hour. A lot of men shop that way—it's shopping for people who hate shopping. This is another reason why stores have to operate differently if they want to accommodate male-pattern buying. For Albert, that wall of preselected, preboxed gifts may start looking awfully good in two weeks.

"How about this jewelry store?" he asks when we're a few paces away from Tiffany.

I hadn't even noticed this one before. The windows are large, which doesn't feel particularly jewelerlike. And the first thing you see is color, a kind of pinky-mauvey-rosy shade that predominates. It looks girly, and not in the best way possible. But there in the window, nestled among the swirls and swaths and swoops of fabric, is jewelry.

Inside we find a horseshoe of display cases, all down around mid-thigh level, meaning they're not the easiest things in the world to ex-amine for fully grown men who don't yet feel inclined to bend over or to sit at the little benches before the cases.

Across the cases we face a pair of middle-aged women, extremely pleasant of face and form, wearing pastel-colored fuzzy sweaters and so forth—not at all the stylish keepers of the crown jewels we encountered at the more glamorous shops.

"Hi, ladies!"

"Well, hello," they reply, more or less in unison. Nobody will confuse this store with Tiffany or Cartier. Or the discount place, for that matter, if only because it's hard to imagine any male wandering in here searching for the key to the front or back door. This is an interesting concept, a jewelry store aimed only at women shoppers.

"Wow, pink lights *and* flowers," Albert says under his breath.

"You think this would be forbidding to a man?"

"Gee, this is what a jewelry store would look like if Hallmark decorated it."

On the other hand, the prices here are moderate, perfect for the woman buying for herself or another woman.

"Is there anything we can show you gentlemen?" a clerk asks.

"I'm not sure I can fit my knees under that counter," I say, eyeing a fancy little bench.

"Oh, it's really comfortable," she says.

"Yeah," I reply, "but you're not six-foot-four!"

16 A Man and His Mall

CAN A GUY love a mall?

The short answer is no, judging by the behaviors we've seen in our studies. At least they don't love it in the way women do. Some of the reasons for this gender disagreement are obvious. Start by looking at the very composition of the mall—overwhelmingly, the stores are meant for female shoppers. Women's apparel is the number-one category. Men's clothing and shoes are way down near the bottom of the list. Once, malls frequently included stores selling books, stereos, TVs, toys, sporting goods, items that at the very least gave men something to idly browse. It's no coincidence that the only popular mall store bearing the name hardware is Restoration Hardware, which trades in furniture and accessories, and where the closest things to actual hardware are drawer pulls. These are marvelous stores, but go into one and try and buy a ten-penny nail or caulk or an ax, designed for real use rather than for Martha Stewart.

The mall is a tamed jungle, the retail concentrate of the urban environment—a very weird city, one in which there is little to do but shop, with a roof and a smooth floor and air bearing the scent of candle shops and cappuccino.

You go to a mall to shop. There's nothing tentative or halfway about it. You can't just dart in and out, or merely breeze by on your way to somewhere else. You must drive there on purpose, then enter into the parking dance, and leave your car, and then make your way from the lot or garage into the core of the structure.

All this and you haven't even gotten close to a store where you want to be.

No wonder male shoppers are more likely to be found at strip shopping centers. There you can, on a sudden whim, steer in, park within sight of your destination, and then enter the RadioShack or Barnes & Noble or Home Depot or any of the other spots where guys feel most at home. How men shop once inside a store is how they shop *for* stores, too. Men shop like they drive. They refuse to ask directions unless they are absolutely desperate. Inside a store, it is our experience, men will bolt in this direction and then that, trying to find what they came in for. If they don't locate it relatively quickly, they are more likely than women to give up and walk out. Men typically do not penetrate any given store as deeply as female shoppers do. This instinct alone makes malls challenging, for they are the least time-efficient shopping venue. Shoppers spend roughly 25 percent less time in a city store than in a mall location.

Shoppers tend not to go to a mall when all they need are a few very specific things. The mall is for shopping as an activity unto itself, something that most men have yet to embrace. In one store we studied, which sells apparel to both sexes, males shopped only half as many racks as women did. And while men's clothing can be found inside malls, most of it is sold in environments designed mainly for women shoppers. It's at the Gap, where it has become increasingly challenging just to figure out which clothes are for women and which are for men. Or it's at department stores, where menswear is typically off in some remote region.

Men's apparel is still recovering from casual Friday. Historically, men favor uniforms, be it jeans and a Steelers jersey or a Brooks Brothers suit and wingtips. Male apparel shopping once consisted mainly of closet replenishment—replacing garments that had worn out. As casual Friday spread to business casual for every day of the week, the men's fashion industry reeled. In a study for Dockers, we captured video of how some men shop for trousers: They find a pair in their size (whatever they've been wearing) and head straight to the register, without browsing the rest of the merchandise or trying anything on. The time spent in the section was roughly identical to what men devote to shopping for beer in convenience stores.

A similar pattern, one that varies according to region—strong in the West and Midwest, less so in the East and South—is the acceptance of dressing down for men: the high-tech zillionaire who does most of his clothes buying from the Land's End catalog, the entrepreneur who spends on cars and boats but never on custom-tailored suits and handmade shoes. My father owned good shoes, casual shoes, and one pair of sneakers. He bought four suits a year and changed his clothes as soon as he got home at night. I live in khakis, soft cotton shirts, and rubber-soled shoes. The custom of dressing for the arena of work has disappeared for many men.

While some department stores still do a decent business in men's clothing, mostly the business has left the mall. The success of a chain like Men's Wearhouse has occurred in freestanding stores, where men are more likely to go. Smart brands follow men to wherever they're shopping, which is why retailers such as Tractor Supply and Farm & Fleet now sell lots of apparel. "The brands will sell to us stuff they would not sell to Wal-Mart, but they ask us not to advertise," a Farm & Fleet manager told me. "They are scared of their other customers figuring out where else the shopper can find their stuff."

In this very mall, there's a Brooks Brothers store and a few department stores with menswear, but that's about it for anything other than sportswear. There's exactly one men's shoe store, and it is perhaps the sleepiest shop in the mall. But there are nine stores selling sneakers. Guess where men find fashionable footwear these days?

It's interesting to note the single category of apparel that *does* seem to lend itself to male participation, and, in fact, domination—sneakers.

There's an entire generation of American males who have all but abandoned the traditional shoe, by which I mean something made at least in part of leather, usually brown or black, appropriate for wearing with what is quaintly still thought of as "dress clothes." If you're reading this book (as opposed to playing a video game), you probably remember shoes. You may even have worn them yourself once upon a time, and perhaps wear them even today sometimes.

Go to the mall and attempt to shop for these accoutrements of yore, and you may have a challenge on your hands. There are still a few men's shoe stores to be found, of course, but fewer all the time. Invariably, they are among the emptier places in the mall, too. You can just walk in and sense that life has passed them by.

At what point did footwear meant mainly for athletic activity become America's shoe? It's a perfect match, sneakers and the United States of America—the youthfulness, the vitality, the casualness and egalitarianism. Europeans, wearing their old-world, highly constructed, uptight (literally, and straight-laced, too, in some instances), leather numbers sneer at our childlike belief that sneakers are entirely appropriate for all occasions, from the playing field to the office to the mall. In fact, one of the most dramatic differences between malls in North America and Europe or South America is how they sound: There, the ambient noise is the clacking of hard heels on flooring; here, nothing but the odd squeak of rubber soles.

This is one of those trends that was fed from all directions. We experienced a generation of oldsters who maintained their health and disposable income well into their seventies and beyond. They stepped out of the world of work and responsibility and into a kind of second childhood. With what footwear did they take this step? Look around—men and women who would never have been caught dead in sneakers, who came of age at a time when sneakers were thought inappropriate for any nonathletic activity, came to embrace them, for the obvious reason—they feel so good. Combine the rubber bottom, the soft top, and then the miracle fastener, Velcro, and you've got a perfect shoe for the golden years. (It's beyond irony, how our eldest citizens have embraced not only the athletic shoe but also the rest of the active wear costume—sweatpants and sweatshirt, garments blissfully devoid of zippers, metal fasteners, and finite dimensions, and rather held up by elastic, such a forgiving friend to the expanding waistline.)

While that practical embrace of sneakers took place from the aged end of the spectrum, a similar evolution was happening from the opposite extreme. Now it's the old-fashioned shoe that has become the special occasion footwear, while the sneaker is the default item—what most of us wear, given the liberty, even when athletic activity is the furthest thing from our minds. Look around and see—we men have dragged our juvenile getups into maturity, our sneakers and T-shirts and jeans and baseball caps. There was a time when the costume worn by a child and an adult were pretty much distinct. That time is over.

The traditional men's shoe industry was blindsided. It didn't understand how the little sneaker section, which used to exist over in a corner of the shop somewhere, was transformed into a fashion monster that has now overrun everything else in the store. It gave rise to settings where men, women, and children shop for shoes together. The male-only shoe store is one more example of how the traditional masculine preserves are being wiped out, like so many other animal habitats the world over.

The domination of sneaker style is all but complete. Stores organize the merchandise by activity—where once we each owned a single pair of sneakers, now we need different types for running, basketball, cross-training (whatever that is), climbing, and then a pair for wearing when performing no activity at all. The comfort and informality of rubber bottoms has extended fully to all types of shoes, so that even the dressiest styles are connected to the ground via soft, cushiony gum rather than hard, slippery leather. The cowboy boot, America's manliest footwear, once upon a time, in the West and elsewhere, is out of vogue, replaced by the casual boot with a bottom that looks like the tread on a truck tire. Even sandals now are simply sneakers with open toes. You can go from the humblest pair of no-name discount store sneakers for six bucks to the Prada pair for $350, and they're still sneakers.

The retail trade used to have a term to describe the role of men in shopping expeditions: they were called "wallet-bearers." Today, even that supporting role is mostly gestural, since the woman is either paying from her own wallet or sharing the load, making the question of whose wallet pays immaterial. Men in the mall are secondary figures. They come to wait.

But how they wait! This has become one of the most poignant issues in all malldom, the matter of what to do with the men while shopping takes place. We've photographed scores of husbands, boyfriends, fathers, and significant others—loitering, lingering, lurking, hovering, cooling their heels in every conceivable posture. Department stores are particularly inept at accommodating these shopping second bananas. You'll find men perched on the narrow edges of display tables, leaning against walls, sitting on the floor next to their equally glum children. The men and the children are found in identical straits, bored out of their skulls but with nothing better to do than wait for the womenfolk to wrap it up. Video arcades—further juvenilization; nothing for a mature man to do.

Men are pathetically grateful for even a bench here and there, maybe a comfortable chair out of the jet stream of moving shoppers. These furnishings are especially important to have near stores that men abhor to enter. We once studied a mall where a ledge suitable for leaning was immediately adjacent to a lingerie store on a day when push-up bras were on sale. The ledge was fully occupied from one end to the other by males, several of whom passed the time by studying (closely) the women entering and leaving the store, and loudly commenting on their need for the garments in question.

So—woe to the mall that doesn't provide a place where women can park their husbands. At Envirosell we call these "human parking lots." We encourage retailers to think of them in terms of the amount of time likely to be spent there.

It's downright undignified what men are made to go through because mall planners fail to recognize the most obvious fact about shopping—that it is a social activity performed by couples and families, wherein the female takes the lead role but all others must be equally catered to and cared for. In other countries it's even worse. We have a terrific video clip of a woman strolling into a department store, trailed by her husband. She stops, points wordlessly to a chair in the corner, and urges him into it, depositing her bags at his feet. It resembles nothing so much as a woman leading her well-trained dog. In a French cosmetics store, we witnessed a man trying his best to keep up with his wife as she bounced from one counter to another, until he finally gave up—and began strangling her, ever so gently, in an effort to get her to stop. At Diagonal Mar in Barcelona, there's a rest area with couches, giving the men a place where they might actually nap, which is maybe the best solution of all. I feel sure that some enterprising mall management firm is going to develop a concept in which men might pay a little extra but find room to sleep, watch TV, read, even work on computer terminals, while their wives shop. There's already something close in a Toronto mall—a "shoppers' club," called Embarq, where members (who pay an annual fee) can come to park their weary selves. The setup is ideal—there's an area for men (or women, but they don't make nearly as much use of it) and, next to it, a place where kids can work off their excess energies, meaning that Dad can half watch the little ones while watching the game, and Mom can shop in peace.

The gender patterns and attitudes we observe while watching shoppers are stereotypical, true. And the stereotypes don't always apply, because men's mall behavior varies according to age.

Not surprisingly, the younger a male is, the better he likes the mall. Older men are less likely to enjoy *any* form of shopping. Their material needs have declined, especially for anything you can find at Abercrombie & Fitch. The mall doesn't do much to lure the older male shopper; in fact, it does its best to keep him away. The middle-aged male shopper, meaning the baby boomer–age cohort, is headed in that same direction: this guy has never been crazy about shopping at the mall, and age will make him even less inclined.

But the Gen Xer has an entirely different view of the place. The younger male shopper was of the first generation for whom the mall stood for freedom from parental control. He was in the first wave of mall rats. Boomers were taught to scorn the mall for all its suburban prefab lameness. But there's a whole generation who got their first wild taste of independence at the mall. It's where they were dropped off on Friday nights by Mom and permitted to run free (within limits)—to shop, blow their allowance, and socialize themselves into adulthood. For these guys, the connotations of the mall are mostly positive. For them, the mall is real.

17 Who Is Your Dad?

WE'RE approaching an increasingly rare find in malls these days, maybe one that will disappear altogether before long: the record store.

Stop a minute and stand still. Look inside the window. No, look *at* the window, and what do we find? Nothing. Clear, unobstructed glass. Freshly cleaned. No streaks. (Ammonia and newspaper—only way to go.) We know this is a record store because the sign above it tells us so. But the window itself is unadorned by a single thing to alert us as to what form of commerce is being committed here—it serves honestly and earnestly as a transparent means through which to see inside. That's the first mistake.

What do we see inside? CDs, of course. But we don't see the actual silvery discs—we see the clear plastic boxes in which they are contained. The awkward, brittle, generic-looking, cheaply hinged containers that some wizard of retail nomenclature dubbed the "jewel case."

Nothing gemlike about it. It's hard to imagine a less engaging, less inviting package—it's a plastic box with an uninteresting surface and an annoying tendency to crack into shards during normal use (usually after falling under a shod foot). It does the job of holding the CD and keeping it safe, I suppose, but as a way to display the object in a retail setting, it leaves a lot to be desired.

Mall shoppers of a certain age will recall its predecessor, the LP sleeve. It had several advantages over the CD case, primarily its size— a foot square. That alone provided an ample canvas for telling shoppers loud and clear what was inside. It gave the performer and record label the chance to make an artistic statement from twenty paces away. You can hardly *see* a CD cover from that distance. Now tell me about the impact it has on us standing out here in the mall, looking in. From our perch the nearest CD is around twenty-five feet away. It looks slightly more intriguing than an aspirin bottle.

So—big news, a manufacturer has fallen down on the job of retail presentation. Record labels today are dismally bad at many of the things they're supposed to be doing, so this particular failure should come as no surprise. They are in deep trouble lately, most of which they blame on pirated song downloads available via the Internet, thanks to the now-defunct Napster network and its successors. I think the failings of the labels and retailers set the stage for what technology has wrought, and there's plenty of evidence right here in this (or any other) music store.

This window is badly employed even by mall standards, which is saying a lot since mall store windows tend to be *so* underutilized. There are many reasons for that fact of life. Due to the structure of retail chains, window displays are designed by specialists and contained in loose-leaf binders stored in a central office somewhere, intended to work equally well in every setting, meaning they don't work particularly well in *any* setting. They're not created with an actual site in mind, and so they don't make any allowances for who will be walking by, or from which direction, or under what lighting conditions.

The other reason for lackluster mall windows is a philosophical one, a decision that's been made by nearly every national retailer, so it's practically a pillar of the mall aesthetic: The principle is that from outside a store, you should be able to see in—*far* in. It's why most mall stores don't have solid doorways or defined entrances to mark the threshold between *out there* and *in here*—you can so easily drift from the corridor through the wide-open entrance, almost without meaning to or even noticing. All appealing notions, right?

There's a practical, dollars-and-cents aspect to this, too—efficient design. Because mall rents are high, and because maximum exposure to the corridor is the goal, stores would all like to be wide and shallow; however, many are bowling alleys, narrow and long. In those wide-and-shallow stores it is easy to see clear to the rear wall. This would seem to be an ideal setup—it eliminates the need for the chain to mediate the shopping experience. Why tell shoppers what's inside the store when you can just stand aside and let them see for themselves? Thanks to the absence of brick and mortar or concrete walls inside this mall cocoon, we've been given the possibility of near-total internal visibility. So why put anything in or on the window that might obstruct the shopper's view of the goods?

Well, I can name about a dozen good reasons. The bowling alleys are always trouble. It is tough to get people to the back of the store unless you train them to visit the mark-down fixture at the back, or you put something strong enough visually to tickle their interest. We call that strategy using a mandala—the traditional big altar at the back of Buddhist temples.

But for now let's stick with this CD store. What does it gain by leaving the windows empty? It allows us to see inside. What do we see? Rack after rack of clear plastic boxes. Is this making your mouth water? Does the glint of a plastic box automatically get you excited for the latest from U2 or Christina Aguilera or Tony Bennett?

This is what I was alluding to before—CDs may be a superior medium for storing and playing recorded music (though even that's open to debate), but the LP sleeve was infinitely better as a means by which to display and explain what was inside. It was an ideal and much-beloved package. Labels and artists exploited that admirably—by the 1960s, it wasn't enough to offer buyers a pretty sleeve, it had to contain goodies like photos, lyric sheets, posters, and other bits and pieces of information and whimsy. It became part of the overall package you were buying, and while the record itself was the main event, the rest all became treasured frills.

Maybe the labels didn't realize? Or maybe they did, but didn't care? Either way, the result was the same—they made the fatal decision to package the considerably smaller CD by simply shrinking the LP sleeve. In the case of reissues, that's literally what they did—they took what was designed to be a foot square, collapsed it, and called it a jewel. Did no one notice that what had been a big, bold, and eminently visible poster suddenly was transformed into a postcard? That didn't stop the record industry.

A bad decision by manufacturers usually translates into bad news for retailers, and this was no exception. Here's one result: As you walk by this record store, unless you are already desirous of buying music, there's nothing to goose you into that frame of mind. In every other store in this mall, there's at least a chance that you'll walk by the window, glance up, see a pair of jeans, or a barbeque grill, or a suitcase, and you'll think: *Hey, I just remembered—I need one of those!* Whereas this music store window will probably tickle no such consumerist gene. If there were a poster or sign or other graphic in the window, or if you could gaze into the store and see an actual record cover, you might suddenly exclaim, *Hot diggity, I keep meaning to get that Rolling Stones greatest hits collection, and there it is!* If you started out intending specifically to buy a CD today, you will enter this store, of course. But is that the only customer the store needs to attract? What kind of world would it be if people bought only the things they really needed, only the things they have on their sensible shopping list? A grayer, duller, infinitely poorer world—poorer especially at the bottom line of retailers. A store is supposed to try and make its goods irresistible.

And this is why conversion rate, which is an essential measure of a store's performance, can be misleading. One way to evaluate store health is to see what percentages of shoppers convert into buyers. The higher the number the better, as a rule. Roughly 70 percent of the people who enter this store will buy something, which could be taken as a sign that the retailer is doing a good job. In fact, just the opposite could be true—maybe the store isn't attracting enough shoppers inside its doors, which would result in a too-high conversion rate. It should be working harder to draw more shoppers in; even if the conversion rate falls, sales will have risen.

So: You look inside and see many, many racks containing something shiny. There are a few posters of recording artists up on the walls, but these too are badly deployed—they're mounted flush against the wall, meaning they can be seen properly only if you're standing there facing them head-on. If these were angled slightly outward, to face the front of the store, they might actually be visible from outside, thereby serving a dual purpose. Owing to the shallowness of the space and the glass facade, the entire store effectively *is* the window display. But a very weak window display.

The funny part is that this very record store chain has an outlet not so far away, on a teeming and hyper-busy city street. Rather than being unipurpose, like a mall corridor, that avenue supports many users with many reasons for being there—office workers rush by next to messengers on bicycles next to a few meandering tourists, all amid the usual urban hubbub of taxis and noise and the controlled chaos that is urban existence. In this crowded but untouristy part of the city, most people rush. Some are on their way to the store, but others are rushing past. For the meanderers, they risk being run down like roadkill. How does this outpost of the same chain handle the window thing?

In a completely different way, as you might have guessed. In the city, it's impossible really to see into the store, because each window (and there are several—it's a corner location) is devoted to a different popular recording artist. Now, this isn't purely a matter of chance—these windows get huge exposure, making them valuable real estate, so the record labels pay the store to be featured in these displays. The windows are a profit center in their own right. But they also function well for the store itself. Every window has got something different going on—a huge picture of Eminem's scowl, next to some hip hop diva, next to a constant loop of Weezer's new video. The scale of everything is high impact—they all fill the windows with heads somewhere between three and five times as big as yours. Meaning big eyes, meaning you'll look. Plus, befitting the rocking merchandise, the colors are jarring.

The city store works harder at bringing people in, at jogging the mental shopping list of every passerby, at announcing to the world which piping-hot, right-off-the-presses compact disc the store has just gotten in stock. The mall store announces only that there are CDs inside, should you wish to purchase one. Big difference.

All the actual selling of the consumer is being left to the labels—to their mass-media marketing campaigns, for the most part. The danger, of course, is that all the marketing in the world can't overcome a bad store. Plus, that approach takes a lot of the fun out of shopping. It takes away the motive for the kind of retailer one-upsmanship that used to make shopping such a heightened experience, and still does in other settings.

Let's go in and shop for CDs.

"Hey, how are you?" I greet the clerk, getting the jump on him. I'm the only shopper here.

"Okay!"

"Good!" I cry.

The first piece of actual merchandise that attracts my attention once I'm fully inside the store is . . . a sneaker. Two of them, in fact, two empty sneakers inside a clear lucite cube, which sits atop a plain gray pedestal. There is, also inside the cube, a small white card with type on it, clearly some form of explanation for the shoes. The problem is that the card protrudes from beneath the sole, meaning that it is, let's see, around waist-high on your average adult. And not tilted upward for easy viewing. So picture it: gray pedestal, clear lucite cube, two sneakers, little white card down at your belly button. You actually have to bend over to read the card; I don't care how good your eyes are.

This, believe it or not, despite all the evidence of poor design and planning, is an example of an excellent thing that malls and mall stores could do easily and abundantly, but almost never do at all: cross-promotion. The simple notion that there's a certain amount of overlap among customers of one store and another, or one type of merchandise and another—in this case, between music and sneakers. Who buys music? Who buys sneakers? Young people.

"Hey, can I see those sneakers?" I ask.

"Well, we don't sell those."

"How long have they been there?"

"About two months."

"I don't get it, do you?"

"There's a music magazine that's running a sneaker promotion. It's the urban connection, you know?"

"Who decides where this sneaker goes? Is it corporate?"

"Yes. . . ."

"Even in the Manhattan store, it's at the same place—front right," I point out.

"I didn't know that."

"Except in Manhattan, front right is at a staircase that goes down to the lower level, whereas here it's at the display of top twenty DVDs. Do you think that makes a lot of sense?"

"The sneaker? I guess so. People do look at it."

Good enough for me. This store features a technological selling tool that has made music dramatically more shopper-friendly: Computers that allow you to audition (over headphones) any cut on most of the CDs in the store, just by flashing the jewel box under a scanner and selecting your song. Record stores of old employed listening booths in which you could hear the latest tunes before making your choices. Then this selling tool fell by the wayside. I imagine it got to be costly. Flash forward a few decades and digital technology brings back a worthy vehicle for the enhancement of shopping. You can browse through a book in a bookstore; you should be able to sample recordings here. On this particular setup, according to the sign above the gizmo, you can hear songs from around three hundred thousand titles, all of which have been downloaded into a server.

"And," the clerk says, "soon you'll be able to see trailers for around thirty percent of the DVDs in the store."

"Do you think records are worse than they used to be?" I ask.

"You mean the recording quality?"

"No, the music. For instance, albums used to have around ten songs, and at least four or five were ones you liked, so roughly half was good and half was filler. Whereas today, because a CD can hold so much music, you're getting like three or four good songs and a dozen just so-so."

"There *is* more filler out there," he says. "You get a good mixture, but then again the market is oversaturated with artists."

"Hey, who is that playing now? It sounds like the Kinks from around 1967." I'm pulling this out of the air.

"No, it's Wilco. One of the best records of the year."

"Whatever happened to D'Cuckoo?" I ask. "Do you remember them? They issued one fabulous CD. It was an all-women rock-and-roll band."

"Who?"

"D'Cuckoo."

"I know the name, but I don't know what it was. That's the problem with the market—here one day, gone the next. That's music."

* * *

It's not just the music store that does windows so poorly, I should point out. In fact, the rest of retailing has fallen almost as low, visually speaking, thanks to the mall. But the worst part is how the mall aesthetic has now infected the urban shopping experience. For if a national chain has the preponderance of its stores in mall settings—which most chains, by necessity, actually do—then the mall window treatments will also be deployed on city streets, where (a) they don't function well, and (b) they degrade the only place left where store windows actually have some life and style left in them.

Take Gap, for instance, not wishing to pick on the chain but finding it impossible to resist. The mall window calls for a few mannequins, spaced at regular intervals, without anything else to stand between the window shopper's gaze and the innards of the store. It's bland, it's uninteresting; and yet it's how most mall windows look, and so it's not jarringly bad. But Gap does its Fifth Avenue flagship store in much the same style. It's how the chain's visual merchandising czar enforces order and organization. As a result, there's a big stretch of suburban blandness blighting Fifth Avenue, totally surrounded by old-school retailers such as Bergdorf Goodman, Tiffany, Gucci, Henri Bendel, Cartier, and so on. The Gap is reasonably well trafficked, in part due to the fact that the area draws so many tourists who may well be comforted by the presence of this mainstay of mall retailing. Maybe to orient themselves in the midst of so much urban hubbub, they gratefully enter this oasis of pale woods, khaki trousers, and mellow Motown piped in through the sound system.

But there's a cost—a little bit more of the cityscape has been claimed by white-bread retail style. Up the street is a huge H&M, a chain (even though its windows are quite a bit hipper than the Gap's, and the store's a lot more crowded, too). Nearby is Club Monaco. All up and down Fifth Avenue and other great urban shopping districts you find outposts of mall-dominated chains. It's taking a toll. The city invented the store window, and now it has returned in some uglier but more efficient form to kill off its father. To call these windows dressed is an overstatement.

✿ ✿ ✿

A few stores away from the music shop we come upon a window sign reading: WHO IS YOUR DAD? To be fair, I should say that this takes place a week before Father's Day, but this makes the sign no less obscure. Is it meant to raise questions of paternity? It's in a store specializing in maps and globes and gear for the intrepid traveler, which does nothing to make the sign's meaning any clearer, at least not to me. It probably seemed very clever and intriguing back in some corporate conference room, where it was unveiled by the visual merchandising agency honchos to the executives whose job it is to sit around in that conference room and make such decisions. Out here in the real world, though, it makes zero sense.

Technology made posters and especially big, lush color photographs a lot easier and cheaper for retailers to come by. With that, dressing the windows made a sudden turn—for the worse. It became quicker and simpler to hire a designer to come up with some fancy graphics and then print a bunch of them in Asia, where printing is cheap, and then decree that they be slapped into store windows and on walls from coast to coast. It used to be somebody's job to step into a store window and dress it—to decorate it and fill it with merchandise in a (one hopes) eye-catching manner. There still are window dressers here and there—in Manhattan you'll find them in the best stores, and everywhere else in America you'll find them in the smallest ones. But in between those extremes, windows are now dressed long distance. They're one-size-fits-all.

18 *Malls of the World*

THE modern-day mall may be an American innovation, but it has gone completely global—from Kuala Lumpur to Dubai, from Tokyo to São Paolo. It's peculiar how the idea has morphed: Birthed in the United States by suburban development, cheap automobiles, and land, malls in other places are interpreted through local culture, customs, and needs. Examining the mutation of the concept is one way of looking at the mall's DNA. Iguatemi, a huge mall in São Paolo, Brazil, is a good example of what I mean.

First, some context. São Paolo is South America's largest city. Imagine L.A. sprawl and traffic, with Chicago's industrial base. Pollution and crime are major issues. The city has more private helicopters than anyplace else in the world. Billionaires scoot over traffic, while ordinary citizens may need three hours to get from one side of town to the other. It is not a pretty city. The tall buildings downtown look as if they are melting as the facades have been eaten away by the potent combination of sunshine and dirty air. In spite of everything, it is a great city for business, and it's the center of Brazil's shopping engine. The locals call themselves Paolistas. They work and play hard. I have an office there.

In the early 1990s, we were the subcontractor to an American firm doing branch bank development for Banco Itáu. The American agency lasted about a year and left. Envirosell was asked to stay, and we now have ten years of experience working for Brazilian banks, supermarkets, a huge local brewer, and multinational consumer product companies. Since many grocery stores servicing middle-class markets are in enclosed malls, we have an ongoing relationship with Brazilian mall developers. We learned quickly, no matter which industry we were working with, to discard our North American lens. Brazil has been described as Belgium inside India, in the sense that it has an affluent middle class surrounded by mind-blowing poverty.

It was very helpful in understanding how Brazilians shop to start with banks. In Brazil, big banks are literally big. A typical Itáu branch has more than one hundred tellers and a machine gun tower in the middle of the banking floor. Large segments of the population have no bank accounts and limited access to a postal system. Workers will cash their paychecks and pay rent and utility bills through the bank where their employer does business. A busy branch can feel and sound like a crowded railroad station.

Historically, Brazil manufactures mainly for domestic sale, and many Brazilian conglomerates are vertically integrated. Banco Itáu manufactures its own ATMs, computers, and office furniture. It builds and manages apartments and housing subdivisions for its employees. It is privately held, and the family that owns it must have more than one helicopter. They have never offered me a ride. Brazilians have taken First World innovations and reinvented them to suit their own needs. While the branch bank and shopping mall are recognizable to the foreign eye, they are distinctly Brazilian mutations.

From across the street, Iguatemi mall looks like an Art Deco monolith. The huge, ornate doorway must have been beautiful in the construction drawings. As in many mall designs, the ornamental entrance is unrelated to the entry patterns, or to the demographic profile of who enters where. There's limited walk-up traffic through that grand door.

Design culture loves building triumphant gateways that often can be appreciated only by the policeman directing traffic from across the street. As at many locations serving a high-end market, most of the important users slip in discreetly through a side door. That entrance typically has no charm or aesthetic value.

In Brazil, with its major crime problems, the mall serves as a gated commercial community. At Iguatemi and every other enclosed mall and bank, the first thing you notice are the security guards. These aren't the usual aging rent-a-cops hired to control teenage mall rats. These guys are hard-eyed, aggressive, and ostentatiously armed. They provide what the streets do not—safety.

The presence of police at the doorways and in the concourse turns the mall into a semiprivate club. At Iguatemi, while the stores are attractive, the real action is strolling down the concourse, and it isn't just teenagers you find there. This is a social setting that no American or European mall can duplicate. I am glad I've come to this mall in my dotage; if I'd been here in my twenties, I would have fallen in love every ten minutes. In many cultures, the middle and upper classes dress up to go shopping. While the designer sweat suit is acceptable attire, and you do see belly shirts, Iguatemi puts the general fashion coefficient of any American mall to shame. The social pressure cooker is evident in poses and active eye contact. In a country where many people live at home late into their twenties, the mall is a meeting place for working adults. Many companies run lunch-hour shuttles from their headquarters to the mall.

In North American malls you can be anonymous and lose yourself in the crowd. At Iguatemi, there seems to be the expectation that you will bump into your neighbors, workmates, and possibly your best friend's gorgeous cousin.

The mall as gated community works at being a complete shopping solution, something the American mall might examine. Beyond the supermarket, the corridors leading from the parking lot are lined with small service businesses—watch repair, a locksmith, travel agent, dry cleaning, even a Laundromat that will wash, dry, and fold your clothes while you shop. These shops may not pay major league rents, but they service shoppers and animate underused space.

The retail mix here has only a few names an American audience would recognize. C&A, the European version of JC Penney, is one of the anchors. There is a cross section of global knockoffs trying to ape Gap and American Eagle. In some of the small fashion houses, you find high-end dresses and accessories, bought at season-end closeouts in New York and Miami, transported across the equator to meet the start of the appropriate season launch. There is a distinctly high-end section of the mall signaled by a change in the quality of the concourse seating and a large, aged but sumptuous Oriental carpet in the courtyard.

Brazilian malls are loud. Some of it is because the corridors and concourses tend to be narrow. In a hot climate, stone and tile flooring helps keep the mall cool, but they also amplify the cacophony. The biggest difference is the sound of footwear. In the United States, the rubber-soled shoe reigns everywhere, especially on shopping trips. While some American women may wear high heels to the mall, they are a minority. American women have learned to feel stylish in sneakers. At Iguatemi, the echoing clatter of feminine footwear is pervasive. High-heeled sandals, spike heels, and mules go with the miniskirts and short shorts. The voices, too, are louder, to compete with the clatter and also to announce one's presence. You can't hear the jukebox playing in many people's heads, but you pick up the cadence and swing in the walk.

The contrast between Brazil and Japan could hardly be greater. Safety is not a concern in Japan. Street crime is almost unknown. Japan has an efficient and widely used public transportation system. Public safety is not just about facts, but also about perception. Unlike anyplace in North America, it is common in Japan to see young children commuting alone across Tokyo to school. The early morning and afternoon subway trains are crowded with schoolchildren aged seven and up, all in uniforms. The youngest travel in small packs, and as they age the packs only grow. In that safe world, the role of a mall as safe haven is unnecessary. Japanese kids can comfortably range far afield, and they crowd the hip urban shopping districts.

There are elegant malls in Japan, including a new one across the street from Tokyo Station called Maru-Biru. It is part of a large office complex, where numerous buildings share the same name, or nearly so. Like all Tokyo street names and numbers, the mall defies logic, and I had a hard time even identifying it from the outside. The mall anchors a shopping strip between Tokyo Station and Ginza, the major shopping district. It's a little sterile and lacks animation. That mall focuses on young, single, employed women, and at lunchtime it rocks, but still the scene is very corporate and restrained.

Japanese consumers vacillate between two opposing impulses. They can be extremely frugal and practical. But they also exhibit a fevered obsession with high-end products and brands. The Japanese are forever looking for a bargain. Relative to the United States, everything from housing and transportation to beer and vegetables is expensive. The meeting of Japanese prudence and luxury shopping tastes creates retailing and business anomalies. In stores, two examples stand out.

Don Quixote is a popular chain in Japan. The origins of the name are a mystery. The name is not used in the Western form, but rather translated phonetically into Japanese and presented in Kanji. It is the Japanese equivalent of the American Dollar Store, or the German chain called Aldi (now found in some U.S. communities), only bigger and with a wider range of products. Often stuffed into aging multistory buildings, the stores are warrens selling everything from canned goods and household products to apparel, home appliances, and electronics. It is easy to get lost. The price promotion signs look hand-done and are everywhere you look. The store presents itself unapologetically as a maze, which is its charm. The Japanese love it for the discounts. The perception is that nowhere is anything cheaper than at Don Quixote.

Another stop on the search for a low-cost shopping fix is a new store in Tokyo called Three Minute Happiness. The copy on the sign outside reads—Just Three Minutes/Enjoy Shopping/A Happy Feeling. It's a retail vacation featuring broad aisles and a simple arrangement of wildly disparate merchandise—"stuff for living," as it is described, arranged not by category but by price. You can find cosmetics, notebooks, housewares, toys, all just paces away from a coffee and ice-cream bar, where you buy a coupon from a vending machine and present it to a human server. It's a store conceived and designed to deliver a cool, pleasurable, highly organized, 180-second experience in the midst of urban madness. Nothing is expensive, everything is fun, and it's all in your face. With small cosmetic samples at ¥100 or ¥200 ($1 to $2), it's a shopper magnet. Both stores play to the consumer's love of value in completely different ways. They are radically different flowers springing from the same root system.

At the other end of the Japanese consumer spectrum is the love affair with luxury brands. Many such brand names do huge business in Japan. Oscar de la Renta, Calvin Klein, and many others license their names to Japanese stores and product manufacturers.

Historically, there is a unique signature to Japanese design, from the brushwork on paintings to the simplicity and grace of ancient buildings and the richness of Japanese textile design. That tradition has influenced Western design for more than 150 years. While you still see that history in twenty-first-century Japan, the best examples of high-end retail are in distinctly foreign settings, such as the Hermès, Prada, and Louis Vuitton stores in Tokyo.

Around the corner from the Imperial Hotel, where I stay, is the new Hermès store in Ginza. Mornings on my way to Starbucks, I pass the crowds waiting for the shop's ten o'clock opening. White-gloved security guards keep the docile hordes in line. It is a lovely store where product, display, and architecture are unified.

How do you explain the particular fervor many Japanese have for high-end brands? It surpasses what we see even in the United States and Europe. It is especially curious in Japan, which has struggled with economic stagnation of almost two decades. Japanese families endure punishing commutes, long workweeks, and expensive but modest housing. But they spend serious money on luxury products and have an almost mystical belief in their value. Just as previous generations may have hoarded gold coins, some Japanese today seem to believe that a Prada bag tucked in a closet is an investment.

To senior executives at luxury goods firms, the Japanese devotion to designer labels is a mixed blessing. The companies love the money— the Hermès and Louis Vuitton shops in Tokyo generate some of the largest sales-per-square-foot revenues of any retail location on Earth. A good Hallmark Gold Crown card store in an American mall may do $500-plus per square foot. A great Gap might do $700 a foot. A French or Italian luxury goods store in Tokyo brings in more than $7,000 a square foot.

What worries the European luxury goods manufacturers is the degree to which their native customers react negatively to crowds of Japanese tourists filling the shops in Paris and Milan. To a European snob, there is something distinctly déclassé about seeing your favorite bags getting on and off the tourist buses. Japanese customers are right to suspect that some products are being deliberately withheld from stores that serve the Japanese market. Some high-end shops in Paris and Milan limit the number of bags they will sell the individual Japanese tourist, but will look the other way when a well-dressed European wants to make the same multiple purchase. Outside the Louis Vuitton store off the Champs Elysée in Paris, Westerners are often approached by Japanese tourists asking if they will make their purchases for them.

As you leave the central urban core and make your way to the residential suburbs, the retail excitement and innovation drop off. The shopping centers serving much of the middle-class Japanese market are unassuming on the outside and aging on the inside.

Nara is a bedroom community of Osaka, Japan's second-largest city. It's home for teachers, middle-aged salary men, and Japan's increasingly visible retiree community. Nara is also one of the centers of Japanese Buddhism. Sprawling temple grounds, carefully groomed and maintained, attract thousands of tourists and pilgrims every year. To serve that trade, Nara has Palace Hotels, conference facilities, and expensive restaurants. Beyond the temples and facilities for tourists, the commuter line bifurcates the community like a noisy brook. Like much of Japan, Nara consists of densely packed pockets of housing surrounded by small farms. From the windows of the mall you see rice-field landscapes right out of the sixteenth-century—surrounded by pint-size strip shopping centers, modern bridges, and train lines. It is a weird vista.

The traffic on the narrow, two-lane roads approaching Nara Family Shopping is backed up for almost half a mile on the sunny Saturday afternoon we visit. Even from afar the mall looks to be more than fifteen years old; on the outside it is nondescript and the paint is peeling.

There's a line of over thirty cars waiting to park in the tiny lot. We end up appointing a designated driver, who spends the next two hours circling while we shop. While most Japanese shopping centers have parking, a lot of the traffic arrives on foot, since many malls are adjacent to commuter rail stations. Bicycle traffic can also be significant. I expected the Japanese to have developed an innovative bike parking system. They have not. In many locations, bike parking is subcontracted out and a uniformed employee is constantly moving locked bikes around to maximize space.

The commuter Japanese bike is solidly utilitarian and functional. This isn't glam bike country, and so theft is not an issue. The bikes are locked, but any urban American would laugh at the modest security measures, easily foiled by a Swiss Army knife. The basic bike comes with baskets and simple child carriers.

On the weekend the mall is populated by the elderly and young families. For both groups, convenience and proximity are trade-offs for the aging building and narrow selection. Employees' smiles are perfunctory and presentations routine and uninspired. Only the kimono shops have any dignity. The vinyl flooring is worn through in places on the first floor. Even the coin-operated kiddie rides in the concourse look ancient. As in many shopping centers, the escalators have been slowed down to accommodate an aging customer base. In homogeneous Japan, a tall, bald, bearded foreigner is not a common sight. My head brushes the bottom of signs hung from the ceiling. While Don Quixote has a sense of discovery, this place has a faint smell of stagnation. You sense the vast gulf between twenty years ago, when Japan seemed destined to take over the world, and now, where it sits at the edge of demographic and economic catastrophe.

Land is precious in Japan, and malls tend to sprawl upward rather than out. While all shopping involves a series of physiological constants—from how our eyes age to our tendency to be right-handed—the implications differ depending on where you go. The design of the signs and graphics is pure chaos to me—not at all in keeping with the serene Japanese aesthetic we Westerners have always admired. But thanks to a pictorial alphabet, the Japanese see and absorb graphic information differently than we do. The Roman alphabet may be easy to learn, and basic reading skills can be taught at an early age, but our system is not efficient. While a bright American kid can read the newspaper by age eight or nine, a Japanese student gains full literacy two or three years later. Much of their early education is about training visual memory. That ability to compress complex information into a series of symbols drives both the haiku and the richness of Japanese animation. It is also why text messaging is so popular in Japan, where words can be entered phonetically, making it easier and faster to compose. For the rest of the world stuck with spelling out words on a twelve button numeric keypad, we struggle to find a clumsy shorthand. On retail signage, the impact is harsh. The use of graphic symbols is coming, and our evolving mall directional signs and maps are good examples. We want recognizable iconography that is more efficient, and easier and faster to read.

Japanese malls are modeled after the country's department stores. Below ground level is where you find the takeaway food operation. As at many non–North American malls, food shopping is a major draw. For most Japanese it's a daily event, and the mall shops package their wares in single servings. The ground floor tends to be where groceries are sold. The middle floors are for general merchandise, like Target or Wal-Mart, with a mix of smaller merchants. The top floors are for restaurants.

The crowding in Japanese shopping is polite and mannerly—however hurried a person is, there is an acceptance of the pace, a resignation to the waiting. I am always surprised at the order in this country, from people all taking their lunch breaks at the same time to the controlled body movements and postures. As you walk the streets, you can pick out the Brazilian-born ethnic Japanese who have returned to the motherland. Their hips swing, the stride is longer, and the shoulders move differently.

It is not surprising that outside Japan, the Japanese tourist is a shopping machine. Much of the problem Japanese retail faces is the perception of ordinary citizens that they are not being offered what they deserve. Japan continues to innovate in developing consumer products and electronics. Yet we have seen few homegrown retail concepts translate elsewhere. American and European retailers have come to Japan with mixed results. Sephora and Boots, the English drug chain, have come and gone. McDonald's, Gap, Eddie Bauer, even Carrefour, the French hypermarket giant, are all struggling in Japan. The Japanese mall needs to reinvent itself and become more relevant in the twenty-first century. Given that Japan is aging faster than any other First World nation, we are looking for leadership on serving seniors. The shopping mall is one place it has to happen.

❊   ❊   ❊

Spain and Portugal have gone through remarkable transformations since the deaths of dictators Franco and Salazar. The countries have skipped fifty years ahead into the twenty-first century, having had the chance to examine what the rest of the developed world did right and wrong.

The most successful fashion chains in the world today are Zara and Mango. While Zara has a few locations in North America, Mango is an unknown in this part of the world. Amancio Ortega, the founder of Zara, comes from northern Spain and has built a retail organization that functions in seventy-plus countries around the world, selling inexpensive yet fashionable apparel. Both stores, but particularly Zara, are staples in non-American upscale malls across the world. They have set the bar for fashion with rich merchandising and lightning-quick responses to the marketplace. It spots trends quickly and exploits them to the max. Jennifer Lopez gets seen in some designer outfit, Zara copies it and has it in stores less than two weeks later. Both chains have dealt the traditional department store industry a serious blow.

The key to the store's success is the degree to which it gets its customers to buy at full price, a concept that has almost disappeared in the American market. Its high-fashion, modest-cost positioning trains you to buy it, if you find it, because two weeks from now it not only will not be on sale, it will be gone forever. The chain manages to get the right product to the right place in the right sizes. The stores are well designed. Zara has not flexed its muscle in the United States, preferring growth in easier markets. However, it's only a matter of time before domestic players like American Eagle, Old Navy, and Ann Taylor get a formidable rival.

European mall developers have been making pilgrimages to the Vasco da Gama and Colombo malls in Lisbon, Portugal, for more than five years now. Both malls were designed and built by the Portuguese developer Sonae, which is also a major shopping center developer in the Brazilian market. Vasco da Gama Center, named for the Portuguese navigator, is designed to look like a modern-art rendering of a sailing ship. It is one of the few modern malls built to look good on the outside, based on the premise that a distinctive external appearance will drive traffic and attract interesting tenants. Like the Guggenheim Museum in Bilbao, or the Tate Modern in London, the exterior architecture is part of the marketing effort. The Vasco da Gama Center is what results from a cooperative visionary relationship among developer, government, and architect.

European retail also differs from the American variety due to the history and role of the merchant. In the United States, retailing has always been a middle-class profession. The price of admission is a little money and the willingness to work hard, rather than education or social background. Few MBAs from America's top schools start their careers in retail. American merchant history is about immigrants and outsiders gravitating to retail as one of the few career tracks open to them. That nouveau-riche history is what makes American retail both brash and innovative, while at the same time leaving it vulnerable to staleness as the entrepreneurs give way to the managers and bureaucrats.

On the other side of the Atlantic, the merchant has always had social respectability. Four centuries of purveying products to wealthy aristocrats has developed the European sense of how to sell luxury goods. The Spaniards, French, and Italians are particularly good at it. Prada, LVMH, and Gucci are all merchant brands with long histories. The Brits and the Dutch have long traditions of merchant banking, the middlemen in buying and selling, tying retail into a comfortable, wealthy establishment.

My European colleagues tell me that Barcelona is the second-most

popular weekend destination in Europe, after Paris. It is one of the
continent's most beautiful cities. For those people who took exotic
stimulants in the 1960s, the Catalonian architect and Barcelona native
Antoni Gaudí possessed godlike qualities. His cathedral looks like
melted candle wax, his apartment buildings undulate like belly
dancers. What substances were they ingesting here in the late nineteenth century?

While Paris impresses, Barcelona seduces. One of my favorite stores
in the world is Vinçon, which sells tools, furniture, and household
products. It's visual merchandising plays in a different league than the
rest of retailing. Even its paper shopping bags, which change with the
season, are distinctive and collectible. It is retail theater that may not
be transportable or conducive to chain ownership. Its owner is committed to art and design, and, while the store makes money, it feels like
a labor of love. In the same tradition as our own Restoration Hardware
and Williams-Sonoma, the store manages to help you fall in love with
merchandise regardless of the price.

That is what makes stores like Vinçon stand out. It has managed to
sustain its edge. In a city that's home to Vinçon and other shopping
landmarks, it's not surprising to find interesting malls. Diagonal Mar in
Barcelona is part of a huge redevelopment project started around the
time of the 1992 Olympics. It's designed to be the commercial center
of a district of high-rise apartment buildings and office towers. It gives
residents the opportunity to shop, congregate, be entertained, and
dine in an elegant pedestrian setting.

While the project is still incomplete, it wins both praise and catcalls.
When you drive into the garage, there is a system for directing you to a
parking place. It doesn't always work perfectly, but at least it's a system.
Like Iguatemi, it has a formal entrance, which seems to have no rela-
tion to where most people actually enter the mall. On the day I visited,
the car/taxi drop-off point was piled high with trash. Likewise, the bus
stop across the street was forlorn. The mall's windows are largely
empty, and the paint of the crosswalks is faint.

And yet, the third floor of the mall opens onto a magnificent plaza
facing the surrounding apartment buildings and office blocks. It leads
shoppers to restaurants and movie theaters on the top floor. The mall

offers a broad selection of dining and is open late into the evening. At night it is a very busy place.

Like an American mall, Diagonal Mar is built with two anchors. At one end is FNAC, the French music, book, and electronic superstore that also sells concert tickets. That combination works well; I've seen FNAC mall stores where crowds have gathered early in the morning, waiting for the ticket window to open. At the other end is Sfera, a chain owned by Corte Inglés, the Spanish department group. Neither anchor store is a stellar contributor to this mall. FNAC is an urban format misplaced in a suburban setting. At the mall lease line are the ticket windows and registers, which make perfect sense for FNAC but are not particularly inviting to the passersby in the mall. Corte Inglés has the same problems that many North American department stores are facing—it is a tired concept that has trouble going up against its more nimble fashion specialty store competition.

On the inside, Diagonal Mar looks like an American mall. There are the predictable skylights on the central corridors and common areas. It is the details that make it distinctive. The tile work is unusual. Shopping carts from the mall grocery store are left on the concourse, as customers visit other stores on their way home from the supermarket. There are some long, gently sloping shopping cart escalators. There's a small lounge with sofas and chairs. This is Spain, and so, in spite of the signs, people are smoking everywhere. In one of the common areas, a Volkswagen Golf is being painted according to designs submitted by local schoolchildren. My Catalonian colleagues tell me Diagonal Mar has shifted the axis of the city and taken a blighted area and turned it around.

While malls are an American innovation, a lot of the most interesting development work is happening outside North America. Some of it is fueled by a better combination of government and private funding, but it is also about changing the rules and making the mall a more complete solution to consumers' needs. One thing the American mall must examine is how comfortably to integrate food shopping into the format. Particularly with high-concept, upscale grocery chains like Wegman's and Whole Foods, the idea is not inconsistent with the upscale mall's image. Iguatemi and Diagonal Mar offer customers shopping, entertainment, good eating, and a comfortable environment in which to watch people and socialize. They manage to duplicate the total urban experience, more or less. As the First World ages, the thought of riding an elevator from your apartment to the supermarket begins to sound sensible. In that spirit, I'd take Barcelona and Diagonal Mar over Miami Beach and Collins Avenue, its main drag, any day.

19 *Where the Girls Are*

"IS THIS where you go inside?"

"Yes," says Brianna. "Because this is the entrance that's closest to Pac Sun."

"Does everyone call it Pac Sun?" I ask Britney.

"Yeah."

If you need to ask what Pac Sun is, you've obviously never spent time at the mall with anyone named Brianna *or* Britney *or* Ariel, as we're doing now. It's a chain of stores called, properly, Pacific Sun, specializing in clothing and accessories with a California surfer/skate flavor, lots of T-shirts and hoodies, and the like. If you wonder why it is that a bunch of adolescent girls living in New Jersey are so devoted to the surfer aesthetic, I do, too, but it seems beside the point to ask. The mall, like the city, is capacious, and serves any number of subcultures and even sub-subcultures simultaneously, and without making a big fuss about it. It's the endless and nonchalant ability of commerce to

157

give us what we want without calling it to our attention. Probably we're all better off this way.

"Would you ever shop *here*?" I ask, referring to the big department store through which we've entered.

"With my mom. Not really," Britney says, making a face. The other girls giggle.

"I go here sometimes," says Brianna.

"Yeah, me, too," says Ariel. "I buy perfume here."

"Okay, let's stop a second," I say. We're in a department store, at the perfume counter. This does not strike me as a place particularly well aimed at teenage girls—it feels like the domain of their mothers, perhaps, of middle-aged women who seek (and pay for) cosmetics and moisturizers and paints and fragrances to emphasize and amplify whatever natural beauty they bring to the party—but here we are all the same.

"I wear Calvin Klein," says Ariel.

"I wear Tommy," says Brianna.

"Polo," says Britney.

"Excuse me," I say to the saleswoman who has come over to where we're standing. "About how many of the shoppers in this department are around the age of these girls?"

"A lot," she says.

That's surprising because this counter does absolutely nothing to attract young girls. There's a big lush photograph of a semifamous actress who's on the brink of incipient middle age and is in the news for having borne a child to her much-older actor husband.

"And you girls shop here because . . ."

"It's on the way," says Brianna.

"Do you ever look over there?" *Over there* is the shoe department.

"I gaze, but I don't *look*," says Ariel.

"Yeah, my mom is always the one who goes, 'Aren't they cute?' and I'm, like, '*No.*' "

"So where do you usually go from here?"

"I go to Musicland."

"First?"

"It depends."

"Do you like music more than clothes?"

"Mmm, not really."

"If you had to decide between buying jeans and CDs, which would you choose?"

"Jeans."

"Jeans."

"Jeans. Because it's always better to have more clothes. And you can always go online to get music."

Pac Sun is drawing us in its direction, but on the way we pass Old Navy.

"Would you go in here?"

"No."

"Why?"

"It looks like what forty-year-olds wear."

"Yeah. Older people."

"Like my mom."

"Teachers."

A death sentence.

"Teachers would wear this to school?"

"No. Some of it is too . . ."

". . . revealing. For teachers."

We pass American Eagle, which appeals solely to teenagers.

"Here?"

"I don't wear preppy clothes."

"Me neither."

"We have friends who shop here, but not us."

"Amanda."

"Or Holly."

"We grew out of preppy."

More death.

"Okay, everything so far has just been leading us to here, right?"

We're there. Pac Sun.

"How often do you come to this store?"

"I was here two days ago."

"How many times a month?"

"Four, at least."

"Same."

"Five or six."

"Eight."

Eight visits a month. Imagine if these girls had money!

"You all come Fridays after dinner?"

"Pretty much."

"Then we come Saturday, too."

"What's there to do in here?"

The answer's obvious, but I like hearing it.

"Oh, look at clothes."

"Look at what other people are wearing."

They're still new enough at this to be aware of what they're doing. Twenty years from now they'll all be here, or someplace just like it, but it will be so reflexive that they won't even have to think about why.

"I like the guys' T-shirts. But I would never wear them."

"They have funny slogans."

"Do you always find new stuff? In other words, if you come in again next week will the store look pretty much the same as it does now?"

"No, they'll have new stuff."

This is the challenge for any store catering to mall rats—the kids come back so often that you're forced constantly to change the displays. Otherwise, they get bored and stop coming at all. It's one reason stores need to know how often the regulars return—to see whether the windows and front tables should be changed every week or every seventeen days.

"Now, correct me if I'm wrong," I say, "but this is what you'd call a surfer store."

"Yeah."

"Yeah."

"Yeah, like California skateboarding . . ."

"And what does that mean to you?"

"Well, it's the kind of music we like."

"What kind?" I'm thinking: *Surf music?*

"Rock."

"Punk."

Oh, right, *that's* surfer music today. Not the Beach Boys.

"Like tell me who, specifically."

"Get Down Boys. Blink-182. Adema. Linkin Park."

"Jimmy Eat World."

"When you watch a rock video, are you noticing what clothes people are wearing?"

"Yeah."

"So you watch a video and see clothes like these, and it's obviously supposed to be some kind of California scene, and you're in New Jersey, but still somehow it registers with you?"

"Pretty much."

"I also shop here because it's different from everyone else. Like today a lot of kids around here are more into rap and less into this kind of thing."

"What do those girls wear?"

"Baggy pants and a tight T-shirt that says 'Baby Phat.' "

They smirk in unison.

"What kind of person is that girl?"

There's a pregnant pause.

"I guess we'd call them *thugs*."

They seem a little uncomfortable with this, but no one can come up with anything better.

"Thugs rather than punks?"

"Yeah. They all have attitude. Bad attitude."

"Where do they shop?"

"There's a store called Against All Odds."

The store names do a good job of differentiating the tribes—you've got Pac Sun versus Abercrombie & Fitch versus Against All Odds. It sounds so young, until you think about Nordstrom versus Versace versus Ann Taylor, and you realize that retail tribalism doesn't end when we become adults. It's just that the signifiers become a little more subtle (to us adults, I mean).

"So you have thugs and preps—"

"Hold on a second. What is preppy today? How's it look?"

"Clean cut."

"Not too tight."

"Everything ironed, and they're like cheerleaders or they like what-ever's popular in music."

"Whatever's in, they like."

"Okay. What other kinds of kids are there?"

"Skaters. Skas. Punks."

"I think that skaters and punks are the same. And then you have thugs."

"Between all those, you have half our school."

"And then you have the rest, the people who just dress normal. Like they all have the same style."

"But you also have people who used to be skaters and then just changed overnight to thugs. Like overnight changed their whole wardrobe."

"Everybody has to have their own place to shop, then, is that right?"

"Kind of," says Britney. "Although my mom shops here."

"At Pac Sun?"

"Uh-huh."

"Interesting."

"See, she does try to do fashion, and she dresses young so she can feel younger, but . . ."

That *but* hurts.

"So your mothers *could* shop here?"

"Yeah," says Brianna, "but mine shops at Old Navy."

"My mother doesn't care anything about fashion," says Ariel.

"So where does she shop? She has to buy something."

"I don't know *where* she shops."

"Britney, what would your mother buy here?"

"She'll choose like the dorkiest thing here."

"Show me what she'd pick."

"*That*," says Brianna.

"Yeah, that dress right there."

"Hey," says Ariel, "I *like* that dress."

"No, not the blue one. Actually the *pink* dress."

"You wouldn't wear the pink one?"

"No."

"No."

"No."

I'm sure this conversation would come as a surprise to the executive suite at Old Navy, since they imagine their chain is aimed directly at girls such as these. In that company's master plan, today's Old Navy shopper migrates tomorrow to the Gap, and then, once she's a little older, all the way up to Banana Republic. But reality has a way of intruding on even the best-laid merchandising plan.

"I'm a little surprised to learn that, in your view, Old Navy is such an adult store," I say. "Would any of you shop there for anything?"

"I do."

"Don't."

"I don't usually find anything in there."

"They changed from when they first started."

"And made it worse?" I ask.

"Yeah."

"Their clothes fit weird."

"Baggier. The jeans got baggier."

"And they've got a funny shape."

"Do you think the jeans are bigger and baggier because there are more older shoppers there nowadays?"

"It's not *that* kind of baggier."

"What kind?"

"More like for rappers."

"Oh! Like thugs, you mean?"

"Kind of."

Another reason to stay away—thugs *and* moms.

"How much time will you spend here in Pac Sun?"

"An hour."

"That feels like a long time. What will you do during that hour?"

"I'll try on a dress."

"And I'll try it on like fifty times."

"Wow. Will you try on stuff from every section of the store?"

"Pretty much."

"Will you buy anything?"

"At least one thing."

"So if you come here once a week, you'll buy one thing a week."

"At least."

"Maybe a T-shirt?"

"Maybe. Or shorts. A necklace."

"How much will you spend? How much is that sweatshirt?"

"Like $40."

"Like $50."

"So you could end up spending fifty dollars every week here?"

"Sure."

"That comes to, what, around $2,500 a year. That's a lot of money."

"It is."

"Yeah, here I sometimes feel things are overpriced. Like $18 or $20 for a T-shirt."

"A plain T-shirt."

"I always go to the clearance rack to see if I can find anything there."

"It's always the first place *I* go."

But lest you go forward under the impression that Pac Sun is the zenith of the teenage girl mall experience, think again. We were discussing the glories of the mall itself when Britney says, "There's only one store missing here."

"What's that?" I ask.

"Hot Topic."

"Hot Topic," Brianna agrees.

"If that was in this mall, that's the first store we'd go to," says Ariel.

"But it's at a different mall, one that's farther away," says Britney.

"What's the best store in the world?" I ask.

"Hot Topic."

"Hot Topic."

"Hot Topic."

Can you imagine finding this kind of unanimity among adult shoppers? This level of rock-solid certainty? Life loses focus as we grow older, and I'm not talking about eyesight here. Teenagers are the ones whose love for the mall is pure and constant and unshadowed by doubt or ambivalence. Do these girls worry about whether their love of buying and owning masks some unmet spiritual need, some emotional dead zone deep inside? No way. Teenage girls may be ironic about a number of things, but stores and shopping and acquisitions and malls are not usually among them.

"They have interesting things that would make you stand out, like express yourself more," says Ariel.

"Clothes, jewelry?"

"Yeah. Shoes . . ."

"Perfume . . ."

"Shoelaces . . ."

"Boots . . ."

"Patches . . ."

"Patches. And that's like the ultimate fourteen-year-old girls' store?"

"Teenager store."

Okay, we're back out of the store and strolling the mall. We come upon Victoria's Secret.

"How about this store?"

"I don't go here," says Britney.

"Too expensive," says Brianna.

"I don't even think my mom shops here," says Ariel.

"This place is more like . . ."

"More like what?"

"Like . . . *lingerie.*"

"Fancier."

"Not like everyday. Not like teenager."

"When did you get that lip piercing?" I ask Britney. Something about walking by Victoria's Secret brings my attention back to how the bodies of these adolescent girls have been adorned, permanently in some cases, by contemporary fads.

"Last month."

"Did your parents have any objection?"

"Not much. My mother said fine, you know, as long as you're going to take care of it, then go ahead."

"I'm not allowed to get any piercings, but I want to get so many," says Brianna. "When I turn eighteen, I'm getting every one that I want."

"My parents aren't that strict about it," says Ariel. "I got my belly pierced for my birthday."

"Your fourteenth?"

"Yeah. But like they don't want anything piercing my face. When I'm sixteen, they said I can get my tongue pierced if I want."

"And you're going to do it?"

"Yeah. My tongue and my eyebrow."

"I want my tongue," says Brianna.

"Why?"

"Because it's fun!"

"How could getting your tongue pierced be fun?"

"It's just interesting. It looks cool when you talk."

"Okay, but do you all imagine someday being, I don't know, adults and mothers, or holding a job? Do you figure someday you'll be a lawyer and talking to the judge with your tongue and lip pierced? And your eyebrow ring? Or do you figure you'll take it out?"

"Yeah, like if I got my belly button pierced and then I was having a baby, I'd definitely take it out, because that would be disgusting."

"How about tattoos?"

"The only thing about tattoos is, everybody has a tattoo nowadays."

"Yeah. Not everybody has a piercing yet."

"But why do you want one?"

"I don't know. It expresses you, I guess."

We've somehow wandered right to the food court.

"Now, usually, we eat."

"Where?"

"Always the food court."

"Not one of the freestanding restaurants?"

"Never."

"Where in the food court?"

"We don't know. That's why it always takes so long."

"This is really most like a hangout, isn't it?"

"Yeah."

"Where, besides the mall, do you girls actually go?"

"Not counting school?"

"Yes."

"Or home?"

"Yes."

"Well, sometimes we go and like walk around our neighborhood."

"And hang out with friends."

"Hang out with friends where?"

"At people's houses."

"But tell me, is there any nonmall, nonhouse place where you can go?"

"Well, there's always the movies. But people don't want to spend that kind of money all the time. It's like $8 every time you go."

"But that's not really hanging out. We go sometimes to the park."

"Sometimes."

"Or to get Chinese food."

"Yeah. We just walk around town and see what we can find stupid to do."

That sounds a lot like most adolescents.

"But other than that or the park, everything you do involves spending money."

"Yeah, that's the way life is. You spend money when you go out, or you stay home and talk on the phone and pay for minutes."

"Do you girls ever meet boys here?"

"Sometimes."

"At the arcade."

"Yeah, that's where you see them."

"And they whistle and stuff. You just keep walking, but . . ."

"Do they whistle because they're too shy to talk?"

"Yeah."

"I guess."

"Is it obnoxious?"

"It's just the way they are."

"I think they're trying to have fun."

"Do you ever go shopping in the mall with boys?"

"I don't know."

"It's weird, because they shop for different things than we do."

"They shop at some of the same places, but they just pick something out and like get it. They don't take the time we do. They don't try stuff on."

"I don't think they have to."

"Yeah, they can look at the label and see it's size thirty-two and the certain length they wear and then just buy it. But for us it can be the right size but everything fits different."

"Do boys go to Pac Sun?"

"Uh-huh."

"Do they spend an hour?"

"No way. They spend five minutes in the store and then the rest of the time just walking around the mall, seeing who they can bother."

"Whereas you girls can spend hours just shopping."

"Yeah, well, we do but we alternate. We shop, hang out, then shop some more."

"We'll get all our shopping done in the first two hours, and then we'll spend the next two hours just walking around and stuff."

"Looking at people."

"Do you go anywhere other than to the stores and the food court?"

"The video arcade."

"To meet boys or to play?"

"To play."

"See, now I always imagined that the video arcade is more of a guy thing."

"I play all the time."

"I do, too."

"I don't waste a lot of money buying games, though, because I need other things. And I don't have time to play video games constantly, like some boys do."

"I play much more than my brother does."

"Who else is at the arcade?"

"Mall junkies."

"Those are the kids who are always, *always* here. Either inside or sitting around on the steps outside the mall, in nice weather. Like the people who no matter when you come to the mall, you see them here. It's like they never leave."

"A lot of them are the kids who live so close that they walk to the mall."

"When did you girls really start coming to the mall?"

"From birth."

"No, I mean coming by yourselves. Not getting here alone, but spending time here without parents."

"I used to come when I was in the sixth grade. That's when I was allowed to spend time here without my mother. She would like drop me off here with some of my friends, and then she'd come back at a certain time to pick us up. Or I'd call her at home when we were ready to leave."

"Do you remember what it felt like the first time?"

"It felt cool to be out somewhere without your parents along."

"Yeah, and you could do whatever you want and buy whatever you want, 'cause you had your own money."

"I think I came the first time with my friend Rochelle, and we went to Pac Sun. I think I bought a shirt, and then we just walked around. For hours."

"Are you girls allowed to go in other kids' cars yet?"

"No. I can go in my brother's car. He drove us here last week."

"What did your mothers do when they were your age?"

"Like, where did she hang out?"

"Yes."

"I don't know. I don't think she was allowed out much."

"Yeah. Like, when they were our age they were pretty much at home."

"Things must have changed, because my mom says 'I'm letting you do things that my mother would never let me do. Like, she would never let me go shopping, or do things to my hair like color it or get it cut or anything like that.' "

"Yeah, when they were our age, I think they were playing with dolls."

"How old is your mother?"

"Right now? She's forty-three?"

"Do you like her?"

There's a lot of nervous giggling at this.

"Sometimes."

"Sometimes I don't really like her, but . . . I guess I'm closer to my dad. I don't know why."

"Yeah. My mom always tries to be my friend, and I get so mad."

As you may have noticed, teenage girls love malls, but as shopping machines they are not without their flaws. For all the time they spend in stores, they have the lowest conversion rate of any demographic, meaning the percentage of female teenage shoppers who buy something is at the bottom of the pack. They are inefficient, in other words, which is not to say that efficiency in these matters is all, or even paramount. Their inefficiency stems for the most part from the fact that they are not in total control over what and how much they purchase. We saw how much preshopping they do—they comb through mountains of clothing, trying on a great deal of it in an approximation of the fashion-show games they may have played in childhood. Then, with Mom in tow, they return to the stores to plead for the items that truly seemed most awesome.

And for all their inefficiency, they (along with their male cohorts) still manage to constitute a $200 billion annual marketplace. If you do the math, every American teenager is the source of roughly $200 a week in total retail purchases. It is true that many American teenagers work—from baby-sitting to taking after-school shifts at the local fast-food restaurants. But most are living off the largess of their families. Their money is spent almost entirely on discretionary purchases. They are, to the economy, pure gravy—they manage, even with limited productivity, to represent a lot of buying power, making them tycoonlike in their contribution to the cosmic bottom line.

They are trendy, impressionable, and emotional in their spending habits, too, easy to reach through the dependable medium of TV. They also possess something their predecessors couldn't imagine: consumer credit. The typical college freshman carries somewhere around $2,000 in ongoing credit card balances, the result of having been importuned on countless occasions since high school. They have time, boundless desires, and money. Is it any wonder that retailers crave their attention?

20 *The Mall Touch*

WHERE do the exhausted, the played out, the spent, the irredeemably mall-sore go for relief?

They climb into a big blue polyurethane-lined coffin, one that's throbbing with slamming, pulsating jets of warm water, whereupon they experience mall ecstasy.

They go to Aqua Massage.

There's a line, so we'll have to wait a few minutes for our turn. It's a good chance to contemplate this phenomenon, which strikes me as a venture that could succeed only in the mall. Maybe that's due to the psychic kinship shared by an enclosed shopping center and an enclosed massage machine. They're both so spectacularly fake that they outdo reality.

If this is your first time, let me describe. It's a large box, maybe the size of a refrigerator. It opens like a coffin, into which you climb, with only your head sticking out. (It's not for claustrophobes.) Then the blue vinyl lining fills with water, and you are pleasurably pummeled in a fashion not previously seen outside the car wash. At no time are you ever touched by a human being, and you keep on all your clothing except your shoes. These are seen as the advantages of this contraption. You pay by the minute, usually somewhere between $1 and $1.50.

It's not a hoax or a con, either—these machines were originally meant to be sold to physicians and hospitals for physical therapy. But they didn't catch on, until some smart businessman got the idea to put one in a mall. Today there are around two thousand in use in the United States. It's a franchise business, meaning that all over this great entrepreneurial country of ours, there are men and women dreaming Aqua Massage dreams of wealth and glory and malls.

You want to go first?

21 *Short Hills or Seoul?*

I PROBABLY spend more time looking at the ceilings and the floors than most people walking around the mall," Ron says.

Ron may be one of the few people I know who has spent even more of his life in malls than I have. He's a store designer—a position somewhere between architect and interior decorator. I like him because he's both the most honest and most cynical mall store designer I know.

He grew up blue-collar in Brooklyn, worked his way through college selling records at Korvette's, graduated with a degree in architecture, but couldn't find a firm that would give him a job. He compromised and took a gig with a store-planning agency. He's now devoted more than twenty-five years of his life to the trade, has his own firm, makes buckets of money, and has not just the inclination but also the right to say what he thinks.

"What do you see up there on the ceiling?" I ask as we stroll.

"Details. Lighting. Lights are extremely important in a mall, be-

173

cause inside the stores it's a totally enclosed, controlled setting, and you've got to make things visible to shoppers, first of all, and then you've got to highlight the things you really want them to notice. No shopper thinks about lighting when they walk through a store, which is how it should be. If you notice it, it's probably because it's either too dim or too bright. Some stores manage this better than others. Smaller ones have an easier job because they have less to illuminate. Most mall stores are built wide and shallow, meaning most of the storefront is right there along the corridor. As a result, there's already decent light coming in."

"How about the big stores? How about the department stores?"

"They've got a tougher challenge. Walk around just about any department store, and you'll begin to pick out the dark spots. You've got a lot of territory to illuminate—say, 150,000 square feet of selling space, and ceiling lights will run you around $25, $30 a square foot. It's a lot of bucks. It's tempting for the store to say, 'You know what, maybe we can just do an acoustical tile ceiling with surface-mounted fixtures' instead of something more powerful that will also be more costly."

"To me, Macy's all seem dark."

"They are. That's because they don't spend enough on lighting. That's what I meant—if you notice the lights one way or the other, there's usually a problem. It's even worse for department stores because their best shoppers tend to be older ladies."

Ron's hit on something there. As we age, the lens in the human eye turns yellowish. Thus, a fifty-year-old sees colors differently than a young person. In addition, those older eyes let in roughly 20 percent less light. Now, most designers of stores and restaurants tend to be young, meaning what they think looks bright enough is too dark for customers middle-aged and older. This is why I have a flashlight key chain—to read the menus in trendy restaurants. Not only are they too dark, but also the young menu designer in all likelihood made the typeface too small for my decrepit eyes.

"Whereas," I say, "when I go into Neiman Marcus, I usually find a big skylight somewhere, and it floods the store with natural light."

"Right," says Ron. "Natural light sends a message—it says we spent some money. It's ironic, that sunlight is more expensive-looking than electric lighting, but it's true. I have no idea why. It doesn't make a bit of sense."

Nowadays everybody's getting skylights. They show up in most newly constructed suburban homes, even the midrange models. The new Wal-Mart prototype uses skylights!

"What else are you looking at, besides lights?"

"I'm looking for impact. I want the store to tell me what it is."

"Do you mean first impression?"

"I want the store to begin talking to me even before I know exactly what particular things I'm going to find inside."

"Show me an example."

"Let's go see the J. Jill store."

J. Jill is part of a significant trend in American retail, wherein some catalog houses are going into the bricks and mortar store business. L.L. Bean, Coldwater Creek, and even REI, the outdoor store, are all examples. L.L. Bean's outlet in Maine is on the top-ten list of tourist attractions in the state. The firm's move into shopping mall country is a very big step. What makes the transition interesting is how a brand so well developed and focused in two dimensions translates into three, and how the successful catalog customer service model changes once the interactions are face-to-face.

A J. Jill catalog is a romance novel's interpretation of how a beautiful, mature female artist might live: walks on the beach, a studio flooded with natural light, the soft textures of a weaver's loom. All the models are over thirty, there is some sexy gray hair, and all the waistlines are gently concealed. The photo layouts are brilliant, and the clothes are soft and romantic, definitely not urban.

"Okay, here we are. What do you see?"

"First, this very soft curtain. No other store in this mall uses fabric at the doorway. In this case it sets a nice tone, and it is a very distinct entrance. There's some topiary up here and a little stone thing on the entrance floor. You're getting some variety in terms of surfaces and textures—the same way the catalog uses texture to evoke the lifestyle. So you are being made to recognize that you've crossed the line from out there in the mall to in here, inside the store."

"That's kind of an exception to the mall rule, isn't it?"

"Kind of."

"Is there a downside to doing it the other way—the usual way?"

"Several that I can think of. For one thing, you might not want every visitor to the mall inside your store. If you're selling high-end goods, for instance, that could be a negative. Which is why, as a rule, the fancier the store, the more definite the line between inside and outside."

"This isn't a fancy store, though, is it?"

"Not at all. But they still have taken some trouble with the entrance. I think their typical customer is a woman who is fairly style-conscious. So it should make what I was talking about before—some kind of specific impact on that woman. Look, once we step inside there's a little fountain here, so we get a sonic hit, the trickling water, plus some soft music. The whole effect slows you down, and that's good, too. There's something very feng shui about what they've done. You get a good, positive, relaxed feeling from the environment itself. It's not casual and noisy, like a store appealing to young trendy buyers. It doesn't have loud music and rock videos on TV monitors and bright lights and all that stuff. But it isn't haughty high-end luxury either—it doesn't say stay away unless you've got a lot of money to spend."

"What does it say, then?"

"I don't know exactly, except that it's saying something—you can tell that much from when you walk in. The point isn't to say everything all at once. In fact, you want to tell a story over the course of the entire store, not just in the first six feet. There's something to be said for starting out a little mysteriously. With luring people inside and letting them discover what you're about."

"I try and tell retailers that all the time, but it's maybe the hardest idea to impart. Part of shopping is discovering. It may even be a very important part of its appeal. It feels as though it's tapping into some primordial instinct we have for hunting or gathering—we like the actual process of finding things. When we enter a store for the first time, our senses are fully alert and our eyes are moving all over the place. We're sniffing the air, and our ears are scanning for clues about what kind of place this is. That's part of what makes shopping a fun thing to do. It's what distinguishes one store from another."

"The merchandise doesn't really do that, does it?"

"Less and less so. Stores used to have strong personalities, and they expressed it through merchandise. Bloomingdale's sold one kind of thing, while Bonwit's sold another, and Lord & Taylor another, and Macy's something different from all those. Today you find the same brands, the same designer labels, in all those stores. It leads to a certain predictability."

"This store seems to have some personality, though, doesn't it?"

"It does, in a weird way. For instance, most designers would do all the walls in white, for a simple reason: It shows off the merchandise better. It makes it pop."

"What colors are these, a kind of taupey shade, right?"

"Yeah. We store designers would all look at that and say it's dangerous because it doesn't highlight the clothes as well as it could. And all the graphics are what I would call organic—there are pictures and other things hanging on the walls, but they're not photographs or posters of the merchandise, which is the way most stores would go. They're not selling goods, they're creating a mood."

"Why is that not what most store designers would do?"

"Because in the end, the store and everything in it are intended to do one thing—sell goods. It can be beautiful, but if it doesn't help the store to carry out its main function, is it good? I don't think so."

"What else do you see?"

"The fixtures look like they were chosen by a decorator rather than by someone who designs retail interiors. I'm talking about these bamboo tables, for instance. Or those baskets. Look at that nice, antiquey-looking lamp. A woman might have that in her dressing room at home. Nothing here looks like it came from the usual sources for store furnishings. Everything's been tweaked a little."

"What would it all look like if it were done according to the rulebook?"

"White walls. Light-colored wood fixtures, maybe, or just plain chrome racks and so on. Ceiling-mounted lights. It could be dressed up from there, but there would probably be less stuff to distract your eye from the clothes. On the walls, there might be photos of models wearing the actual goods being displayed nearby, with copy making the connection. A bit more institutional-looking, less like some individual person went out and picked the furniture and wall coverings for this particular store. And maybe there would be less mood overall, but the merchandise would be more prominent in the mix. Here, the room itself got all the attention, while the clothes are displayed in a very simple way—almost like whoever designed this didn't know much about presenting merchandise."

"What do you think the effect of this store will be on the shopper?"

"I imagine she'd want to stay in here a little longer. It's a nice room. It's a break from the rest of the mall. It actually feels like the kind of boutique you'd find in the city, on a street downtown maybe. That's why I like this, because it will give the shopper an experience that's different from most of what's out there, and it's someplace that begins speaking to her in a distinct voice the second she walks in."

"Is there any reason *not* to do a mall store this way?"

"Maybe some shoppers will look at the store and be turned off by the boutiquey feeling, and they won't wander inside. If this were a big, bright typical mall store with the usual, durable fixtures, it might be more welcoming to your average shopper."

"But then we'd like it less."

"Exactly."

"The world of visual design in stores seems to have declined. Retailers aren't spending the money they once spent, and they're not taking any stands in what they do. All the decisions are being made in a central office, and made so they can work in every store equally well, meaning they've got to be somewhat generic. They no longer see the store itself as a kind of stage on which the merchandise is presented."

"It depends on which store you're talking about, but for the most part you're right. Back in the old days, in the 1960s and 1970s, you had big retail executives with big egos, and they sought out creative designers and hired them to come up with distinctive looks. The designers were like hired guns, and they went back and forth depending on who had hired them for what. Then, the trend shifted and the retail chains began hiring in-house design staff. It was a smart move for them because it took the best designers off the market and away from their competitors. Designers ended up exposed to less, and they were influenced by less, too. As a result of all that, the design world became static and even a little stale—you had one client, and you came up with something, and then you just worked on refining that. It took some of the edge away. That's why the whole world of retail starts looking the same."

"Less one-upsmanship among you designers."

"Yes. We were just hired by the fashion division of a huge Korean corporation. They own a chain of stores throughout the country. They're positioned somewhere between Ralph Lauren and Burberry—they're like the Polo of Korea. And I spent some time there recently, and it amazes me how throughout Asia the brands are all totally formed by American images. The stores, the clothes, all the collateral stuff—the ads, the graphics and visual material, its all blond-haired, blue-eyed imagery. Indonesia, same way. Japan. On the highway, as you approach the big retail-entertainment complexes, the billboards all show people living the dream suburban American lifestyle, with hammocks and golf clubs and blue-eyed, blond-haired families. The Koreans hired us because they wanted to buy what they called 'New York style.' They came to New York from Seoul and interviewed a bunch of firms looking for a representation of simply that. They didn't really know what they wanted, except that it look like New York—like something you'd find in SoHo. They wanted that quirkiness, that style you find there, and they wanted to box it up and ship it to Korea. Which is what they hired us to do."

"And you did a good job of it, too, I imagine."

"The best. Soon you won't be able to tell Seoul from Short Hills."

Okay, so now we're in a fancy department store, in fact, *the* fanciest department store in this particular mall, and we're not in just any old part of the store but in one of the fanciest sections (though not *the* fanciest—that's just around the corner from where we're standing).

Yes, we're standing in ladies' clothing, so to speak. And when we look into the department, we see: sleeves.

Not disembodied sleeves, of course—but the view from this particular spot is of women's suit jackets and blazers hanging in racks, and the racks are positioned in a way that saves space, a result of which is that the sides of the jackets—meaning the sleeves—are what face the shopper. You can tell quite a bit about a jacket by looking at the sleeve, it's true—the color and fabric at the very least—but a jacket must be seen from the front to experience it. This will come as no surprise to the executives of this famous department store chain, and yet somehow, standing here, what we see are sleeves.

"What can be done?"

"Well, there's actually a very simple solution. You could chevron the racks. Angle them, so instead of the shopper looking head-on into the sleeve, they'd see a three-quarter view of the front of the first jacket in each rack."

America's store shelves and display racks would almost universally be improved by making this change. That's because the way shelves and racks are stocked is fundamentally at odds with how people move. We walk facing forward. In order to look directly at a box of cereal or a bottle of shampoo on a supermarket shelf, we'd have to turn and face squarely sideways. But of course it's impossible (or at least dangerous) to walk facing sideways. And so we tend to examine shelves and racks and so on from an angle. If the merchandise was angled to face us, we'd see it head-on.

I could easily devote all the working hours of a week to strolling the retail aisles of America making just this simple change. And believe me, the shopping experience would be instantly improved for all parties, resulting in higher sales and lower shopper frustration.

"And there's another advantage to chevroning. When you angle the racks, you actually eat up more floor space than the other way. So you have room for fewer goods on display."

"And what's good about that?"

"Well, we've tested this with shoppers, and they think it looks like there's more merchandise out there, not less. So you can fill up the selling floor using fewer goods, which means lower inventory costs."

"What happens to sales when they chevron the racks?"

"We measured that. They go up some. Not a huge amount. But there's always a bump."

"So if chevroning the racks would show the jackets off better, why don't they all do it?"

"Well, because of a problem that's widespread in retail but especially so in malls: no storage space. Once upon a time, department stores had vast warrens of stockrooms and storage areas. When these mammoth retail emporiums dominated downtowns, they had all the space in the world for storage and offices and all manner of backroom operations."

"The mall killed that?"

"Real estate prices did. High rents did. Today the pressure is on to make every square foot count. Nobody can afford stockrooms. Everything goes straight to the selling floor."

"And that's why they can't chevron—it's too crowded."

"Correct."

"Is that also why sometimes it seems as though too many clothes have been put onto the racks, especially ones with hangers? They're jammed so tight you can't pull anything out."

"There's been a fundamental change in how the space in retail businesses has been apportioned. Imagine your house with no closets. That's retailing today."

"Even in a fancy store like this."

Every so often I'll get a call from some group asking if I'll testify in court against a big retailer for not being as wheelchair-accessible as the law requires. I reply, "Look, I am very sympathetic to what you're trying to do, but, in terms of the state of retailing, there aren't a whole lot of choices." You build a store today and plan for maximum selling space. You also try and make as much of it accessible to wheelchairs, baby strollers, and shopping carts as you can. The dilemma is how much of your design and construction budget is going to get chewed up by accessibility issues. Yes, there are real travesties out there, spaces that totally ignore the spirit of what the Americans with Disabilities Act is supposed to accomplish. Prada opened a store in SoHo in 2001, and it won lots of praise for its fabulous design. I have yet to be in it when the elevator works.

Retailers are frustrated because they are aware of the accessibility problem. From the designer's point of view, getting the basics right, from ramps and railings to bathrooms and doorways, is hard enough. The store has to do the best it can, and it's our responsibility to point out where it fails. However, making a legal issue of it ignores the most powerful marketplace rule, which is, if you are offended, take your business elsewhere. Store planners, particularly when working with older buildings, have a difficult time complying with the ADA. If you leave enough space for a wheelchair to go from the central corridor to the farthest recesses of the store, you have to leave a lot of empty space between fixtures and racks.

I have been asked to testify as an expert witness on behalf of handicapped shoppers. I have also been approached by big department stores also asking me to be a witness in their defense in ADA cases. I understand both sides of the issue, and so far I have chosen not to get tangled up in *any* court cases, although I am very willing to talk off the record to both sides. When merchants seek my advice on how to deal with ADA lawsuits, I suggest that they confess not only to the 267 violations they were charged with, but to admit that they were probably in violation of the law in about 3,000 other instances, too. And if the law were broadened to make America's stores baby stroller–accessible, the number of violations would be double that. Then, I say, they should explain to the court that they could probably afford to fix fifty of those accessibility problems a year. If the ADA is really going to help, it will be used not to sue businesses but to help them prioritize their violations and fix the worst ones.

"I'm looking at that far wall there," Ron says, "and I can't even see *all* the way through—even though they have merchandise allegedly on display there."

We approach what, on some store designer's computer screen, must have looked like a wall display rack of women's silk blouses. Given the average adult human's eyesight, the display would be completely visible and thereby effective at, say, twenty-five feet. Unfortunately, there's no unimpeded view of the wall from that distance. In fact, you can't see the blouses until you're around five feet from them. There's a lot of merchandise on the selling floor. But at a certain point each display gets in the way of all those surrounding it. The clothes begin to cancel one another out. You find it difficult just to maneuver around everything. And your eye can't keep it all sorted out—it creates a visual jumble. It's not simply unappealing—you are actually incapable of taking it all in, and so you don't.

"What the heck is that red thing?"

Up above the wall rack of blouses, maybe ten feet off the floor, there's a shelf. On the shelf is a big red shiny ceramic something. Behind that is a wall hanging—fabric. Also bright. Yellow.

"It's what they call a design element."

"No, look, it's a vase!"

"Yes, but it's a vase with no practical purpose. You'll notice it isn't actually holding anything. Clearly, it was intended to catch your eye from far away. It's a decorative piece, but it has a job, too. It's supposed to tell you that there's something over here to see."

"The silk blouses that are obscured by all those floor racks."

"These blouses are $200 each. And this rack alone holds about twenty of them. So, that's $4,000 worth of goods hidden from customers. Put yourself in the place of the shopper looking for an expensive silk blouse. Does a crowded rack of merchandise obstructed by a floor display signal 'fancy silk blouses'?

"I mean, are the visual clues we all rely upon adding up? There's not a great big sign that proclaims 'really expensive high-quality silk shirts over here!' Stores speak to us in subtle ways. The way these blouses are presented to the eye has to give shoppers a fair amount of information about them. One formerly reliable clue was this: The less clutter, the more costly. That's the rule in the store itself, or in any given area of it, or on any rack or shelf. At the Dollar Store, you expect to see merchandise jammed into every nook and cranny. Just like you expect to find linoleum floors and metal racks and plastic signs and fluorescent lighting. Whereas in this place you want carpeting and marble and polished wood and a nice, upholstered chair. Beautiful and clean dressing rooms. And a certain amount of spaciousness on the selling floor—it says that the goods are so costly that they cover a *lot* of rent."

We stroll closer to the escalator, where there are . . . more racks. The very fact that these racks are off the selling floor and in the passageway, where foot traffic is highest, indicates that the merchandise on them is cheaper. All the cues are working properly—discounted clothing, so you have to stand in traffic to shop it. But still good stuff, because it's a good store.

"Isn't there something wrong with having discounted good stuff sold within view of nondiscounted good stuff?"

"I think there is. These sale racks attract bottom-feeders—shoppers who maybe browse this store on a regular basis but never or hardly ever buy because the prices are high. Those women see these racks out here, and it's like a jackpot: the goods they covet at a price they can afford. But what effect does that have on the full-price shopper? Maybe she sees the action out here near the escalator and never even makes it farther in, to the pricey stuff. Maybe she buys two sweaters out here instead of one in there, which means the store's not getting the markup it might have gotten. Or maybe she sees the sale merchandise and the cheap racks blocking the way and decides that she'll begin shopping elsewhere—maybe in one of those ultra-high-end Italian designer boutiques elsewhere in this mall. Maybe for her, shopping away from the riffraff is an important factor."

"It sounds like a risk for the store."

"I think you're right. But there's the potential for reward, too, which is why the store does this. On the one hand, you want to take full advantage of the space and of your brand identification. Look at what nearly every luxury brand has done in the past decade or so—they've all searched for ways to sell things to less-affluent customers. There are moderately priced Mercedes-Benzes now. Armani has high-end stores, midprice stores, and stores for young shoppers interested in jeans and T-shirts. Every big-name designer has what they call a bridge line to pull in the younger shopper with less to spend. These stores are no different, and when you consider how department stores are dying out like dinosaurs, it becomes doubly important not to miss a bet. But they have to be careful not to turn their good customers off. The store can be a dynamic space, where more than one thing happens, where today's discount shopper can become tomorrow's luxury customer. But it has to be done in an orderly and controlled way."

"Does this look orderly and controlled to you?"

"Could be. But having so much merchandise on the full-priced floor, and having it within sight of the discount racks, is probably not anybody's big plan. It just happened this way, I bet. Now look up ahead for the opposite situation—where the store proper gives way to the designer boutiques. What they call the vendor shops."

Here's where the identification issues really become complex, be-

cause this out-of-the-way corner is where the world-class labels—
Chanel, Gucci—sell out of little boutiques within the larger store. But
the conditions that prevail elsewhere aren't totally absent here, as is
evident as soon as we get close to the beautiful and expensive-looking
table behind which business is transacted.

"Now, what do you see there?"

"The table?"

"On it."

"Office junk."

"Well put. We're looking into a part of the store where probably the
average garment costs upward of $10,000, and on the table where that
sale is recorded is a slightly scuffed blue plastic three-ring binder.
There's also a $1.19 pen, some blank sales slips, assorted other cards
and pieces of paper, a telephone that wouldn't look out of place in a discount electronics store, and various other items required by the person
who runs this department. Under the table is a small trash can with a
plastic bag liner. Am I missing anything?"

"I think you got it all."

"It doesn't say 'Chanel,' does it?"

"Not to me."

"I guarantee you that when the Chanel executives come through
here to visit, all that stuff gets stowed somewhere out of the way. You
need paperwork and staplers and pens to do business. But why does it
all have to be out here? And why doesn't Chanel provide the proper
tools—like a beautiful leather-bound book, or a silver pen, and an ap-
propriately glamorous trash basket? This stuff belongs behind the
counter in a discount drugstore. You can't really expect the clerk to
leave the selling floor every time she has to make a phone call or order
something or write a letter. And there's probably no meaningful back-
office space for those tasks. But Chanel has to recognize the design
equity in everything—the clothing but also the trappings, the furnishings, and so on. If the salesperson came to work in jeans and sneakers,
Chanel would fire her on the spot. But they don't object to her using
Wal-Mart–level desk accessories."

The details of visual merchandising are critical pieces of merchant
magic. How stores present themselves has become a form of commer-

cial art. Andy Warhol started his career as a window dresser and advertising illustrator (his specialty was women's shoes). I've been in the most exquisite shops on the most exclusive blocks all over the world, and I've witnessed just about everything a person can do to exhibit goods for sale. I've seen artful displays that hush a room as profoundly as anything in the Louvre or the Uffizi. But my all-time favorite retail vignette is still the towering stack of canned foods found in supermarket aisles. Executed properly, on a massive scale, it stops me in my tracks every time. A mountain of peas! An ocean of V8! I look and wonder, How long did it take that clerk to pile up a thousand cans of pork and beans? Were there any shaky moments when the whole thing was about to come crashing down? And how did he feel once he was through, when he stood back to check on its symmetry, and to make sure all the labels were facing the same way? Did it fill him with pride? I sure hope so—I admire the diamond room at Harry Winston and the private couture salons at Barney's. But for sheer retail balls, you can't beat a twelve-foot-tall pyramid of canned cocktail nuts.

There's something about typical mall design, with its straight row of flat storefronts, that discourages shoppers from stopping. Granted, they must stop all the time, otherwise no store would ever be entered and nothing would be purchased. Still, the monotony of the storefront line allows you to walk in a kind of ambulatory trance—you're passing one sheer, absolutely flat wall of glass after another. There's nothing to slow you down, nothing that catches your eye by jutting out into pedestrian space. When you look a few paces ahead of where you are, as walkers normally do, you can just barely make out what's in the upcoming display windows. If there's glare you may not even see that much.

This is what we're faced with in the mall—sheer walls of glass, absolutely even and regular, with nothing to break the plane. The leases demand that each store stop at the same exact spot, and there are severe limitations on what (if anything) can be placed out beyond the wall of the store. We shoppers circulate without even seeing how unnatural this is. Walk down a city street, and there you'll find endless variations on the vertical facade, a multitude of planned or sometimes completely ad hoc deviations from the flat front wall. You need to pay attention, if only so you don't trip over merchandise that's been dragged out there.

Just the other day I was walking by a store specializing in leather bags, briefcases, coats, and so on; a clerk noticed three tourists staring in the window, so he casually sauntered out there to join them in conversation. As I passed they were all standing shoulder to shoulder, pointing at a suitcase. Good retailers do their best to make the storefront as porous as possible, something that rarely happens in a mall. The poignancy of this occurs to me whenever I happen to visit a mall on what they usually call "Sidewalk Sale Day." On these occasions, stores are permitted to bring a rack or two of merchandise out into the main thoroughfare; some malls even allow stores to drag goods out into the parking lot. It's a real novelty, and speaks volumes about our vestigial connection to the street—seeing how the mall attempts to evoke the sidewalk is enough to make you laugh.

Some mall stores do at least acknowledge that important things can happen right at the outset of the store, in the entrance. At both the CD store and the sneaker stores, we see video monitors mounted high, facing the doorway. They try to send their energy and pop culture signifiers out into the mall thoroughfare to snag shoppers. Even better, they're noisy and feature lots of motion and light and color, which would grab your attention anywhere, but especially in the bland confines of the mall. Here, when Jay-Z raps in your face, you notice, whether you like it or not.

Music stores especially have to deploy these attractions judiciously. For instance, we know that a mall's demographics shift depending on the time of day and day of the week. On a Tuesday morning at eleven, you've got stay-at-home mothers and their small children. You may lure them in with the latest Bon Jovi video, but they're not buying 50 Cent. Even earlier in the morning, when the mall walkers are out, the store might do best to blast some Sinatra. Most music stores now sell DVDs, too, so movies can also be screened on these monitors, especially when there are likely to be few music fans in the mall. Maybe by day they could run the new Richard Gere movie on the monitor. On a Friday night, however, teenage tastes rule the mall, and kids are the music store's prime audience.

A sneaker store doesn't have those particular considerations to make. But it does need to maintain its image within the mall, and the music and videos it plays are an important part of that. As America's taste in pop culture has gone urban/African American, kids who have never set foot outside of these middle-class white-bread confines are rocking styles that are straight (more or less) outta the Bronx and Compton. Nowhere in all suburbia does this exist more vividly than in the sneaker store. It's where the latest look to win the imprimatur of Allen Iverson can be had by any tow-headed fifteen-year-old with $100 to spare. Here and the music store are where urban culture manifests itself most tangibly in the lives of suburban kids and adults. Go ahead and laugh— once again, the retail arena is where we all finally learn to get along.

❖   ❖   ❖

We've just come upon the mall toy store. Toys are another category largely gone from the mall. Money is the reason, of course—you need a lot of space to compete in the toy market today. For Toys "R" Us, it makes a lot more sense to build a freestanding store. The mall has gotten too expensive. There are some toy stores left, but they tend to be small and specialized, like the ones focusing on toys for all the little geniuses, of which there are no doubt many. Who has average kids anymore? Today, even kids understand that average won't cut it. This toy store isn't anything spectacular, but they do one thing that no other store in this mall can do: place little windup swimming frogs and remote-control cars out ever so slightly in the corridor, the better to attract the attention of passersby.

"Ron, what do you think of how some stores come out into the mall itself?"

"It's a great idea, assuming mall management lets you get away with it."

"They usually frown on that, don't they?"

"It's in the lease—you either can or can't put freestanding signs out there, for instance, or if you can, they can only be so far away from the wall, and only signs of a certain type, and so on and so forth. Otherwise, you'd have every store in the mall dragging stuff out here."

"I imagine the toy dancing bear gets a little more leeway than, say, a rack of T-shirts."

"I think you're right. It's a form of entertainment."

"Yes, it is. Speaks volumes for the rest of the mall, doesn't it?"

"Well, there's not much in a mall that entertains kids, is there?"

"No, and that's a problem. Malls really try a kid's patience."

"So this becomes the reward, right? A trip to the toy store."

"While Mom is shopping somewhere nearby, I bet Dad and the kids stand out here and stare at the remote-control cars. You could easily kill four minutes just doing that."

We stop and stare at the remote-control car and the swimming frog.

"You have to drive that thing carefully so it doesn't go too far out into the mall, don't you?" Ron asks the grinning teenage salesclerk who's steering the car.

"Yep, otherwise they'll give me a ticket," she says.

22 *Other Venues*

I WANT TO get out of this mall.

When malls came along, it seemed as though they had commandeered all the considerable shopping energy in America. In fact, they did contribute to the downfall and even death of a great many downtown shopping districts, in cities but also in small towns, villages, even in suburbs, which in many cases were as old and venerable and self-contained as any urban district.

But big enclosed malls never really did render urban streets or even suburban strip shopping centers obsolete as places where retailing thrives. In fact, while malls are really good at certain forms of shopping, they're vastly inferior in others.

Take bookstores. They are moving out of malls everywhere, largely driven by high rents. But they also discovered that they have higher conversion rates away from the mall—that more shoppers actually buy something in freestanding stores. That's because in a mall, the bookstore is a handy place to browse around and kill a little time without really meaning to buy anything. Also, today's mega-bookstore usually includes a café, which often is the most profitable real estate in the store. But in a mall, shoppers are likely to get their refreshments elsewhere. So the café doesn't serve its primary function—that of keeping people in the store longer.

I want to spend a few minutes here thinking about how malls compare to other shopping venues. And since I'm a guy, and since I'm now weary of the relentlessly female-driven atmosphere of the mall, I want to start by thinking about a store selling consumer electronics and technology toys. Pretty much a full-service place, where you might go for anything from batteries and solder guns to telephones and remote-control toys to flat-screen TVs and digital cameras. I say it's a guy kind of place because in one sense it is—stores like this have replaced the auto store and hardware store as spaces where a man can roam idly and probably find a few things he wants or even needs. (Whoever has enough speaker wire?) But women buy a hefty amount of the technology on display, so the stores need to attract and work for both genders.

What happens in this store when it's located on a city street, or in a suburban strip shopping center, or in an enclosed mall? Well, in a city, roughly one in ten passersby will stop inside. Slightly more will enter in a mall. But in a strip shopping center, more than four out of every ten people who pass will go into the store.

A dramatic difference, and one that's fairly simple to explain.

In a city, lots of people will pass the store, most of them with absolutely no intention of shopping there. Maybe they're on their way to shop elsewhere. Maybe they're racing back to work from lunch. Even this one in ten figure would be high in, say, midtown Manhattan. Strip centers are, by their nature, destination sites—typically they'll have fewer than a dozen stores, so a high number of people are headed for a particular store.

The gender mix in this electronics store will also be affected by its location. In the mall, nearly four in ten shoppers are female, but only half that many in the city or the strip. Among mall shoppers will be women for whom visiting a techno store is not a high priority—she'll see the window and be reminded that she needs a monitor for her desktop or blank videotapes.

For a store such as this, the prime demographic is males under forty. In the city and strip, roughly four out of ten shoppers are men between twenty-six and forty. In the mall, only 10 percent or so fit that description. This should be seen as alarming news for the mall store, or at least for merchants who need male shoppers. The mall is attracting too high a proportion of males younger than twenty-six—mostly teenagers and under, I'd wager—or older than forty, probably *much* older. The prime group of male consumers is shopping at the strip, which is more its style, or in the city during a lunch break or after work.

City and strip shoppers spend more time in the store. Undoubtedly, this store gets better, more committed shoppers at the strip or in town. In fact, city shoppers usually are in and out of stores much faster than those in a mall, which makes the disparity even wider than the numbers show. It also reflects that in a mall, especially for men, it's tempting to leave a store the second it begins to bore you, since there are at least a hundred more from which to choose.

The difference in conversion rate is significant. More than half of all strip shoppers will buy something, best of the venues. If the store doesn't have exactly what he wants, he may compromise, since there's no guarantee he'll find it elsewhere. And if he doesn't find what he wants, he'll probably find something else he needs. In the city, a similar, but not identical, dynamic prevails—if one store doesn't have what he's looking for, maybe his travels will bring him by another store that will. But maybe not. He'll either buy nothing here and gamble on finding it elsewhere, or, like the strip shopper, he will settle on the next best thing. In the mall, you've got a lot of guys idly browsing, with no intention to buy. Also, it's easy to go from one store to another until you find exactly what you want. As a result, conversion rate in the mall is lower.

✻　✻　✻

The comparative numbers are different for clothing stores, such as a well-known emporium specializing in reasonably priced sportswear for both sexes. In this category, strip shopping center locales are more or less irrelevant—you tend not to find big apparel stores there.

The percentage of shoppers who use fitting rooms is almost identical in city and mall—one customer in five tries at least one garment on. But it's interesting to look at the difference in how often shoppers must wait for dressing rooms. In the city, one shopper in four waits; in the mall, it's four in ten. This isn't necessarily due to crowding—it's because people move faster in city stores than they do at the mall. City shoppers are on the move; mall people are there with no other tasks to juggle. We tend to absorb the velocity and rhythms of our environments. It's not just that mall shoppers are slower. In many instances city shoppers and mall shoppers are the same people. We all go with the flow.

The same velocity applies in transaction time—in the city, average time at the register is one-quarter less than at the mall.

When it comes to apparel, mall shoppers spend longer inside the store than city shoppers do. They also shop more items, and they are more involved in the *act* of shopping. In the mall, they're more likely to look at the price tag and read the label. What's the significance? In part, it means mall shoppers will be more deliberate. There's also the sense that the mall shopper isn't quite as committed to buying anything at all, whereas in the city the same person finds what she wants, examines it, tries it on, and hurries to the register.

Our final grounds for comparison is the outdoors outfitter—the place to go for clothes and equipment for the rugged life (or for people who just want to dress that way). These shoppers spend twice as long in the strip center store as in the mall; they shop twice as many departments and almost a third more items. Nearly half the strip shoppers convert to buyers, compared to around one-third of those at the mall. Strip shoppers are twice as likely to use the fitting room. The strip store gets more couples, the mall more singles. The mall gets more unplanned visits.

23 Scenes from a Mall

I AM A SUCKER for Jackie Chan, it doesn't matter how stupid the movie is. I got hooked years ago by a fight sequence in an appliance store that integrated refrigerators and ovens into the action. While I fall in and out of love with Hollywood actresses, my fascination with Jackie is constant.

I'm giving in to the filmic urge, but only after I feel I've done enough mall talking and walking for one day. That's the wonderful thing about having a cinema this close to shopping—you can build your day around it. It's a fitting reward after an outing of ambulatory acquisitioning—a nice dark place to sit for two hours.

Movie houses are expensive to build, even the bare-bones, thin-walled, cheap-seated cinderblock specimens you tend to find at the mall. But it's usually worthwhile from the developers' point of view. The marriage between the mall and the movie was born of a practical impulse—you were already drawing people to the premises, and there was plenty of parking available, especially at night. In the early days, the mall was the bait that attracted moviegoers. Now it's turned around to some degree—there are plenty of people who come for the movie but fit in an hour or so of shopping.

Mall shoppers and movie fans tend to be the same folks. Shopping and movies are both popular leisure activities. But in the mall the fit has not been properly worked out. Most times, it's hard even to find the theater. There will be a tall sign outside, the mall version of a movie marquee, announcing the films playing. But beyond that, you can walk the entire mall and never see an ad or a sign announcing the presence of a theater. If you don't pass the theater entrance (and it's usually in an out-of-the-way corner), you might forget it's there.

You'd think the cinema operator might want to make it as easy as possible for shoppers to take in a show. If that were the case, there might be a box office within the mall itself, a kiosk or counter where you could learn about what's playing, find the show times, and buy your tickets in advance (or pick up tickets ordered over the Internet). Somewhere in this mall, Hollywood's latest masterpieces are running. But you'd never know it. Nowhere are there measures being taken to turn shoppers into moviegoers—the theater operator isn't distributing discount coupons for early-bird admissions or supersize sodas and popcorn. There are some posters advertising current films—but nowhere does it say if those movies are playing at the mall. There should be a digital sign somewhere announcing ATTENTION, SHOPPERS: THERE ARE STILL TICKETS AVAILABLE FOR THE 2:30 SHOWING OF THE NEW JACKIE CHAN MOVIE.

There *is* plenty of movie-related merchandise for sale in here, but it's all over the mall—DVDs and soundtracks at the music store, movie screenplays and bios at the bookstore, licensed items like action figures and cartoon character lunch boxes at the toy store. Nobody has brought it all together and tied it in with the presence of a cinema here in the building. There should be a major movie presence at the food court. There, as we've seen, everybody's sitting and eating with nothing to look at, not even a window. It's a perfect place for a big video screen showing trailers for what's playing now or coming soon. Food court diners skew young compared with the rest of the mall, so it's a terrific way to reach the prime movie audience.

When you arrive at the theater—once you find it—you come upon a similar lack of retail sensibility at work. This is evident the instant we walk in the door of this fourteen-screen multiplex. Back when theaters showed just one movie at a time, your approach to the building filled you with anticipation. Everybody walking alongside you and every person milling outside in line was going to see the same film. It provided you with a shared entertainment experience that's in short supply today in the land of the twenty-screen cinema and the one hundred–plus channel digital cable TV system. I think this is one reason live sports and rock concerts have maintained their appeal—there's electricity in the air when people convene to watch a single event. Americans today long for that kind of pop-culture communion from time to time. It's a big reason we're all in the mall.

Today, when we arrive, we're split fourteen ways. This is more like an airport than a movie house—everybody is arriving at staggered times with different destinations. At the airport, business-class flyers rush in next to families headed to Disney World beside snowboarders off to Sun Valley; here, some of us are headed to the new animated feature, others are bound for the slasher bloodbath, others for the hot-date movie. We're barely in the same building psychologically. Visitors to the Cineplex and the airport share the same food, time, and bathroom anxieties. We all race from box office to popcorn line, then wander around looking for the right theater. Once we've figured that out, we mill about, waiting for the line to form.

How could this chaos be harnessed? Nobody has ever accused Broadway of being a hotbed of retailing energy, but even there, a few sensible tricks are deployed. True, everybody is there to see the same show, a unanimity of purpose that makes packaging it a lot easier. That is a unique situation, granted, but some of those tricks would translate to the movies. What happens after you've gained entrance into the movie lobby? Almost nothing. You can stand around and look at those dumb cutouts promoting upcoming films. If you're hungry, you join the concession line. Some theaters provide video games, which do occupy a certain number of customers and throw a little profit to the bottom line as well. But the games are aimed at adolescent tastes, so there's a good portion of the crowd that's either annoyed by the noise or will just ignore the machines altogether. It would be a great place for classic video games. Donkey Kong and Ms. Pac Man. As well as a place to showcase video games tied to specific movie properties.

Our research shows that, on average, moviegoers arrive eighteen minutes before their show starts. That's an eternity by retail standards, and they're all in a well-defined space with nothing to do.

Broadway shows usually take advantage of the lull by offering show-related merchandise. This could happen here, too—as I noted earlier, there's no place in the mall where our movie fixation receives any retail expression. But this would be a perfect spot for DVDs, soundtracks, T-shirts, posters, books, action figures, you name it. I'd build a store on wheeled racks, so it could be pulled back against the wall when the lobby's mobbed. Otherwise, this would be a great place to shop, if only because the lobby-waiting experience is so dull.

But let's back up to the entrance. There, a highly practical need is going unmet. We've got fourteen screens, maybe ten movies in all, quite a few of which opened yesterday. Naturally, I arrived knowing what I wanted to see—but what if it was sold out? I didn't have a plan B, and this theater is doing absolutely nothing to help me come up with one in a hurry. I stand in line at the box office with nothing more compelling to do than eavesdrop on the bickering couple behind me.

The cash register experience here is no more linked to entertainment and movie stars than the one at Wal-Mart. All I've been given to look at is a sign up ahead, at the box office, which lists relatively tiny movie titles, even smaller show times, and the price. Standing here is boring and tells me nothing about what's playing on the other thirteen screens. If one is sold out, I'm in trouble: I'll be under big pressure to choose an alternate fast and get out of the way.

Or, let's say I showed up at the theater not completely sure of what I want to see. It happens more than exhibitors seem to realize. Maybe I just wanted to see *something*—that's more likely in a mall than anywhere else. Right now, this theater is doing practically nothing to entice me into a seat.

What would serve me is, once again, the movie trailer. This is one of the truly genius inventions of the cinema business—it's a staple of our lives, and often it's the source of more entertainment than the movie it means to advertise. Right at the theater entrance, a bank of video screens would be entertaining for those in line, informative for those who are still trying to decide, and a good way to attract us back to the theater soon. Best of all, it's dirt-cheap. Somebody could also clip the best reviews from newspapers and magazines and put them up on an easel. We're not necessarily looking for film criticism here—all we want is the plot summary, the movie stars' names, and maybe a quick thumbs-up or -down. Something we could absorb fast. In principle, it should happen in two places—outside the box office and inside the lobby. Art movie houses tend to do this well. I have yet to see it at the mall.

I also don't understand why all fourteen theaters in the complex are the same. They may differ in size, but not in design. On any given weekend, a typical Cineplex has a very predictable assortment of movies—family, teen, guy movies, and date or chick flicks. In your fourteen-theater complex, some number of theaters would, in my plan, be set aside for family and teen movies only. The seating and flooring would reflect the abuse the theater is going to get. They could even be hosed down if that's what it takes to get the Pepsi off the floor. The location of those theaters relative to concessions and bathrooms would also be taken into account. The action-movie theaters would have more legroom; the date theaters would have armrests that fold away and a section of love seats that sell at a premium price.

There's also nothing done to recognize that we're in a mall. Here, for example, you tend to get people who are shopping in small groups—families, or bunches of friends. They attend movies that way, too, different from the usual cinema configuration of an adult couple, or two friends, or single adults. Here, then, a simple thing like selling food to match group size would make a difference. You should be able to get the family meal—two large sodas, two small ones, a couple popcorns, maybe some Raisinets, for a special price. Or even something geared to couples. On Broadway, again, and also at sports arenas, they sell alcoholic beverages. A theater looks the same on Saturday afternoon when everybody's here for the SpongeBob SquarePants movie as it does on Saturday night. Does that make sense? The lighting in the lobby, the amateurish slideshow movie-trivia quiz that runs between features—

nobody is tailoring it to the people in the room. In a world desperate for guerrilla marketing opportunities, the three-dimensional engine that a Cineplex represents is poorly understood.

The movie business is built on the blockbuster, the film that will open huge and then tail off. The theater is getting maybe ten cents out of every admission dollar, which makes all the other sources of revenue that much more important. It's no surprise that the concession stand is a theater's only chance for profitability. But we were taken aback to learn that roughly 11 percent of all customers who get in line at the concession counter step out of line without buying anything. They worry that all the good seats will be taken, or that the show will start, so they bolt into the theater empty-handed. Maybe the line is moving so slowly that they talk themselves out of that big infusion of sugar water, starch, and chocolate they had planned. In every retail setting, some people abandon the line. But nowhere does it happen at anywhere near this level. The movie theater business has a lot of work to do in managing its environment.

A movie's success is indicated by how many people come to see it on the first weekend it hits the theaters. A studio may spend five dollars marketing every seat it sells on that first weekend. The cheapest and most effective marketing medium and audience development point is the Cineplex itself.

Every night of the week, in every movie house in the world, are the loyal customers, the people who are most likely to return repeatedly. Almost nothing is being done to ensure that they return soon. Nobody bothers to collect their names or e-mail addresses, even though they are the industry's lifeblood. There are no coupons for future ticket discounts, or even fliers.

Once the movie ends, you are ushered through the ugliest exit corridor you've ever seen and ejected into reality. You may see a stray poster, or a cardboard cutout to tell you what's coming next July. Whatever dreamlike state Paramount or Miramax has put you into is rudely interrupted by crowds at the bathroom and the rancid smell of spilled faux popcorn butter on cheap carpet.

24 *The Postmall World*

I'M TIRED. I don't think I can go on much longer.

Part of my mall-sickness may be due to the fact that I just polished off my second Cinnabon. (I didn't see the need to mention the first one.) But maybe I'm all malled out. Maybe you are, too.

We've all entered the postmall era. I don't mean that the ones we have are going out of business. We'll still visit them and spend our money there. But as a defining concept, as a relevant institution, as a contemporary form of commercial organization, the mall's heyday is history. These shopping centers will never look as shiny and inviting and wonderful to us as they once did. We're never going to love them the same way again.

Do I mean that the mall is a flop? Maybe. I suspect there was a fundamental flaw in malls from the very start, something that virtually guaranteed that their growth cycle would last just a few decades. Less than forty years ago they were still novelties. We had yet fully to comprehend what they would someday mean to us, how they would transform American retail culture for better and worse. In the boom years, the 1970s and 1980s, a new mall would open somewhere every three or four days. Aging cities and towns quaked with terror every time a new one broke ground, and with good reason, for all it took was a couple of suburban shopping centers to devastate a traditional retail district. Malls were the Godzillas of shopping.

Today, you don't see many malls being built in North America. We're all malled up—new ones succeed only by cannibalizing older centers. We barely replace those that close.

I put a large amount of the blame on the mall's fatal flaw—its lack of mercantile DNA. This is an industry driven by real estate, not retailing. If a mall is in the right spot, it will almost surely thrive. It lives by the axiom that guides all real estate: location, location, location. Beyond opening the doors and turning on the lights, what kind of retailing savvy has the mall exhibited? How has it kept up with and responded to the social and economic changes of the past two or three decades? Ask yourself this: What have been the coolest recent innovations at the mall? The food court? Ferris wheels? In the past, attractions you could find only at the mall kept shoppers interested. In 1990 a new Disney Store could cause a noticeable bump in attendance. There hasn't been a hot novelty for some time. We've had malls in abundance for more than three decades now, and we shoppers have explored all the corners and crevices, every store and pushcart, every Build-A-Bear workshop and rock-climbing wall. Developers didn't plan a future for the mall, and so far none has arrived.

There are examples of developers trying different approaches. In Tokyo there is a "nostalgia mall," aimed at older shoppers. It specializes in the consumer goods they marveled at in their prime. In an otherwise flat economy, the Ichome Shotengai is booming. The mall used to appeal exclusively to young shoppers, who are rabid shopaholics in Japan, but they began running out of money just as the population of elderly rose. It's like a museum of consumer goods. I wish somebody here would try specialty malls with a little imagination. I fear I'm in for a wait.

Two-thirds of America's biggest malls are more than twenty years old. That's not ancient, as buildings go. But the featureless, flavorless architecture of many of these monstrosities will give future generations no good reason to rehabilitate them, whereas we found plenty worth salvaging in aging department stores, railway stations, hotels, and other public edifices.

Strong malls will continue to prosper. Failures may go through two or three incarnations as malls, but then, inevitably, some other use comes along to "repurpose" what would otherwise be a very large white elephant. "Most centers, if they don't make it as a shopping mall, are ideally positioned to be easily converted," a spokesperson for the International Council of Shopping Centers was quoted in a newspaper article, perhaps too candidly. "It's the whole nature of a mall. At their basic heart, they're just a collection of boxes."

The makeovers that succeed are news, and the rest are aging roadside ruins. One particularly American transformation is the mall that undergoes a change of ethnicity. We've always had specialty shopping centers devoted to one or another immigrant culture. Koreatown Mall, in Los Angeles, is maybe the most famous in America. In Atlanta, a failed outlet center first became an Asian mall and, more recently, Hispanic. All kinds of shoppers, not just the obvious ones, are drawn to exotic novelties. As I'm writing this I read that in Charlotte, North Carolina, a failed mall has been taken over by a trio of Vietnamese sisters who have dubbed it Asian Corner, the planned home of retail, restaurants, and groceries to serve the ten thousand Vietnamese residents of Mecklenburg County. I have no doubt that it will also be an attraction to the region's non-Asian residents looking for a slightly unusual mall dinner or shopping trip.

Near Atlanta, the Buford Highway Farmers Market brings live eels, ginger cakes, and other delicacies from all over the world, especially the Third World, to the area's newly arrived influx from Southeast Asia, Latin America, the Caribbean, and Eastern Europe. An estimated 700 immigrant-owned businesses now inhabit what had become a rundown commercial strip shopping center. This did not take place according to any developer's plan but thanks to happenstance and necessity and pluck, the way outbreaks of retail vitality have always occurred. American commerce relies on this recycling mechanism; as one group moves up and out, there's always somebody coming in right behind them—newer, poorer, and boiling over with energy and optimism and resilience. We all know how successive waves of immigrants revitalize residential areas. Less noted is how they bring new blood to aging retail environments. It reminds us how merchandise, bought and sold, has served historically as our primary means of cultural exchange.

The country is dotted with mall repurposing. The Bell Tower Mall, in South Carolina, was taken over by Greenville County and is now County Square, a complex of governmental buildings. The cinema has been turned into a courthouse. Inspired, the nearby Carolina Center Mall is planning to turn itself into a recreation development with athletic fields and an arena, perfect for hosting volleyball and soccer tournaments, and maybe a movie theater, too. The hope was that all this activity would draw kids and parents, enough to support as well a little retail and a few restaurants—the two businesses that once filled the entire mall. The Downtown Mall in Tupelo, Mississippi, was wiped out when another mall opened just outside town. Now it's the city's convention center. In Dallas, twenty-year-old Prestonwood Mall failed and was then converted to a center for telecommunications and Internet companies. Malls are being turned into light manufacturing centers, warehouses—churches have bought a number of failed shopping centers. Westchester Mall, in High Point, North Carolina, was put out of business when a bigger, better shopping center opened nearby. The mall was acquired by First Wesleyan Church and is now a religious complex including sanctuary, bookstore, and nursing home. They call it Providence Place.

Even one of our most culturally significant malls—the Sherman Oaks Galleria, in the San Fernando Valley, backdrop for the movies *Fast Times at Ridgemont High* as well as *Valley Girl*—has been remade. The roof has been removed, and now a townlike complex with lots of open-air street-level activity fills the site. Movie animation studios have moved into a spot formerly occupied by a department store. Overall, the space devoted to retail has shrunk by more than a third.

❊   ❊   ❊

Technology has also taken a bite out the shopping mall. Take your average thirty-year-old today and compare her monthly obligations to those of her mother. The contemporary middle-class American has a lot of expenses that didn't exist a generation ago. Say $100 a month for a cell phone. Throw in another $50 for cable TV. Add $20 or so for your Internet service provider. Maybe you own a desktop computer and a laptop, and every two years you're replacing one or the other, or both; spread that cost over a year and it's another $100 a month. DVD rentals. Download on demand. TiVo. There, you've got at least $300 a month that will never be spent inside a mall—$3,600 a year for each of us. A fair chunk of that money used to go to shopping and restaurants and, by extension, the malls.

Another piece of the puzzle is our relationship to our cars. While we love our vehicles, we increasingly hate driving them in heavy traffic, and congestion is no longer strictly a rush hour experience. Few North America malls are tied into any public transportation system. At what point will the aging First World population walk away from their cars? My mother, at age eighty, plots with her condo-complex neighbors about getting to and from the store when she no longer feels comfortable driving. In Sydney, Australia, the hot apartment complex combines great views of the harbor with an elevator that drops you to a mall that includes a grocery store and delivery services. The mall has to imagine itself into our demographic future and see where it stands.

We baby boomers are in a postshopping mode, psychically speaking. We're not as thrilled as we used to be at the mere prospect of buying, of being in the presence of multitudes of objects, talismans, fetishes, beautifiers, intensifiers, glorifiers, junk. If we needed it, we bought it, more than once. Now we're feeling bought out. We're bored. People in their twenties and thirties always looked slightly askance at our consumption binge. They're not quite as sold on the idea of salvation through shopping. An awful lot of today's middle-class disposable income goes for adventure and vacation, intangibles that nourish something more than Calvin Klein's bottom line. The fact that malls didn't find a way to keep up with the zeitgeist's every twist and turn also explains their overall failure of imagination. Teenagers and children are still excited by the mall, but it's all still new to them, isn't it? Give them time—when you consider all the blandishments and temptations they'll be exposed to, they should become jaded a lot faster than the rest of us. And face it: What's the alternative to shopping for those adolescents? Almost anything that smacks of the outside world and independence looks good when you're twelve.

The fact is, the mall is trapped by its success as a place to bring the family. It has never found a more sophisticated way to envision itself. The food court is a shrine to lowest-common-denominator food—it's pizza and burgers and ice cream and cookies, a menu guaranteed to please any four-year-old. To my knowledge, nobody is experimenting with the mall food court. I could easily see splitting a really big one into two halves—one for juvenile diners of all ages, the other a bazaar of high-quality, higher-priced dining for mature palates. Ideally, the layout would permit you to seat your kids in their food court and keep an eye on them from yours. Keep waiting.

Because some of us are too busy to spend as much time at the mall as we once did, retailing has gone chasing after us elsewhere. The mall has been successfully re-created at airports, for instance. It's a sound notion—especially today, when we're instructed to check in at least an hour before flight time. That means you've got thirty minutes with nothing to do and a limited area in which to do it, since you've already gone through the security screeners. The airport in Pittsburgh has an extensive retail section, and not just junk for tourists—you can buy clothes and shoes. Denver has one, too, as does Reagan National Airport in Washington. Especially for time-pressured business travelers, these airport shops save a few trips to the mall. I could tell that airports were taking this seriously when a national airport manager association invited me to speak at its annual conference. Retailing there has to adapt a little to the location—for instance, shoppers tend to be toting clumsy carry-on bags, so aisles need to be wide.

The Internet bubble has popped, but still this shopping venue represents a dramatic change in the retail landscape. Online shopping plays to the heart of the mall audience—middle-class, middle aged and younger, pressed for time, already in front of the computer every day. The promise of mall as community is being realized at eBay, the flea market of the twenty-first century. There, and at good shopping sites such as Amazon, there's an experience superior in some ways to the real world. Amazon seems to recognize also that the future of any shopping medium isn't based on its popularity with Silicon Valley male geeks, but on how it plays with overworked and overcommitted women in mainstream America. Look at Amazon's most dazzling innovation—one-click buying, whereby, with a single click of the mouse, the sale is rung up and ownership of the goods has transferred from them to you. The world of retail has yet to figure out a painless, graceful way to handle the transaction itself—the cash register experience. Whether you're at McDonald's or Nordstrom, the exchange of money for goods takes place in essentially the same way, and poses the same potential for anxiety, frustration, and unhappiness.

The cash register and the credit card machine look like prehistoric tools—the stone axes of retailing. The basic design of the transaction point hasn't changed in fifty years. Yes, we've added bar code scanners and better credit card machines, but the physical act and even the transaction time is about the same. If anything, the experience has gotten worse because the process has been depersonalized. Even as supermarkets have experimented with self-scanning stations, a significant percentage of customers refuse to use them. They want the final opportunity to see what they are buying before it disappears into a shopping bag. Technology has tried to solve the transaction issue with something called source tagging, an advanced version of the bar code we find on most packages. A source tag reader can tally everything in a shopping cart without the merchandise even being unloaded. The practical problem of ensuring that every product coming into the store has the correct source tag has proven difficult to manage.

Internet retail is still hampered by the fact that you still can't really *shop* online, if by that we mean look at and touch vast amounts of merchandise. But the Web is a great place to buy certain things, such as books, music, videos, software, appliances, electronics, toys, drugstore stuff, anything for which you have a fairly sure notion of what you want. You can info-load at the store, select the exact thing you desire, then go buy it online and save the taxes and, sometimes, shipping, too, or do it in reverse, info-fuel online and make your decision in-store. But if you enjoy, for instance, the experience of exploring a bookstore in hopes that something will catch your eye, you'll have to go to a real store. I buy some books online, but two-thirds of my purchases still take place in stores. Most clothing will continue to be bought in stores, but you can replace the staples as needed online. If you live in thirty-four-waist, thirty-four-length, pleated-front, cuffless, relaxed-fit khakis from the Gap, you can easily buy them online. A lot of us have found our personal uniforms—jeans, button-down cotton shirt, whatever—and those items you can buy just as well online as in stores.

Malls have for the most part remained clear of much Internet influence. Some have tried creating a virtual mall online, but it's expensive to wire every store to permit online shopping with real-world pickup. Some malls have websites listing stores and phone numbers, but that's a fairly low-tech use. At Fashion Show Mall, in Las Vegas, they use the Internet to attract a steady stream of tourist-shoppers by setting up a bank of stand-up terminals and offering free minutes of online access. Last time I was there, the place was packed with tourists checking their e-mail.

The cell phone also may play a role in the future of the mall. In Europe and Japan, cell phones seem to work everywhere, while in the United States phone users are often driven outside or to odd corners of the mall for good reception. The cell phone as a shopping aid allows contact with your buying adviser; a photo-equipped phone can bring that person right into a store aisle or dressing room. But if the phone doesn't work inside the store, the point is moot. At Envirosell, we have started to track the phone conversations that happen in stores and their apparent effect on buying decisions. It's remarkable how predictably the conversations begin:

"Honey, I'm here at the mall, what did you say you wanted?"

All technology and tactile experience aside, the principal condition that is strangling the mall is time. The bulk of the mall's core customer base, particularly the women between thirteen and fifty, has never been busier. A time-poor customer has brought about the success of two postmall shopping center trends.

The first is actually the postmall version of a premall suburban fixture, the strip shopping center. These have always tended to be somewhat random collections of stores, mostly locals. It was where you'd find the dry cleaners next to the Italian deli next to the car wash next to the beer distributor. Today's version is sometimes called an "affinity center." These developments are bigger than their predecessors, and more sophisticated in design and layout, although the storefronts are still visible from the roadway, and parking is still right out in front. The innovation is in the selection of stores. There will be no more than five or six, all national chains, usually big, so-called "category killers." They'll all appeal strongly to the same well-defined demographic group. It's like a mall for people who are sick of the mall. It's for people who are saying: "Look, the mall is okay as a place to spend an afternoon with the family once every few months, but I don't want to go there every time I have to shop. There are 107 stores in our mall, four of which I actually frequent. So I'm much happier to find a shopping center that's got Barnes & Noble, Bed Bath & Beyond, Best Buy, and Starbucks. Or, one with Home Depot, Staples, Old Navy, and Blockbuster Video. I can buy 90 percent of what I need there, and my trip takes no time. Parking is a breeze. And I don't have to deal with all the noise and nonsense. I've seen a hundred Disney Stores already, and I don't ever need to see number one hundred and one. And besides, I *always* thought the mall was bogus."

The second and more exciting innovation is what have been called Main Street developments, or "neo-villages"—twenty-first-century attempts at re-creating urbanesque (or is it small-town?) American shopping. Mashpee Commons in Massachusetts is a good example. These take up less room than the typical mall, although they're expansive in their own way. There are lots of stores, many of the same ones we find in malls everywhere, and focusing on the same basic categories.

But these centers do their best to look like communities. It's genuinely fake—some include phony facades that extend upward two or three stories, although the store itself is all on one level. They're made to look like that staple of old-school retailing, a storefront with the owner's quarters upstairs. But these are so charmingly artificial that they seem theatrical, almost like movie sets. Unlike at the mall, some genuine thought has gone into the architecture here, an attempt to make it pleasing to the eye and human in scale.

Developers have created entire little villages this way, complete with pavements and streetlights and vest-pocket parks. On each little grid of streets you find big national retailers right next door to locally owned restaurants and even some service businesses, like the shoe repair or a post office. You never lose sight of the fact that you're in a manufactured simulation of a real town or city shopping district. It's all a nod to Disney, but again, you can't help but admire the effort. Some of these even include some housing nearby.

There's nothing particularly new about this. All over Europe, you see mixed-use developments that include shopping malls. There, the complex is also likely to include a good supermarket, one with an extensive selection of prepared foods to go. That's the kind of thing that encourages daily after-work visits to the mall. On the outskirts of the development may be small, locally owned service businesses, a drop-off pick-up laundry, the dry cleaner and key maker and hardware store. There could be some office space. There will surely be a residential component—maybe apartment towers or housing clusters or both. A hotel is also a possibility. And very close by will be mass transit—a commuter train stop perhaps, or a bus line. It's remarkably villagelike, appropriate on a continent that perfected the small-town form of social organization long before our country even existed. Recently, I saw an odd version off the highway between Milan and Genoa, where somebody built an outlet mall as a fake town complete with false facades and plastic moldings. It sits in a fog belt for much of the year, which makes its appearance even stranger.

Main Street complexes have their charms, but they are also much more efficient than the mall as a place to shop. You can hit and run— dash into a single store and be out of there in fifteen minutes. You can arrive with the desire to visit three stores, find yourself attracted to one or two more, visit those, and still get out feeling as though you've accomplished everything in a compact time frame. Or, you can go thinking that you'll kill a few hours, visit some stores, wander the streets, get in your dose of people watching, and experience it that way. I think these urbanesque layouts speak to some ancient part of our souls, the love of browsing and exploring and window shopping. Discovery is one of our most satisfying emotions. "There has to be emotional content to the shopping experience," said Limited Brands CEO Leslie Wexner, speaking on the subject of a neo-village mall near the company's Columbus, Ohio, headquarters. I think he's right.

Nearly all of these involve one thing—pedestrians walking on con-crete pavements and asphalt streets, with real curbs, and out in the open, exposed to wind and rain and cold and heat and all the rest. In one sense, it's just a mall without a roof. But that may be a critical dif-ference: Ripping the roof off this sucker may be all that's required to liberate shopping and keep it real. After so much time inside the air-conditioned bosom of the enclosed mall, breaking out sounds a little like heaven.

There's something poetic about all this, isn't there? The mall was a little *too* hermetically sealed for our tastes. This trend renews my faith in humanity.

Okay—what did we miss? Not a thing that I can tell. And we can al-ways come back, right? The mall isn't going anywhere, but I am. I've had it for today. You can stay if you want. I'm going home.

Endcap

Now WHERE the hell did I park?

Acknowledgments

TO MAKE this book possible, Lucia and Willie Tonelli had to give up their father, Bill, for many weekends in a row. I would like to thank them for their sacrifice.

Alice Mayhew, David Rosenthal, Emily Takoudes, and Scott Gray at Simon & Schuster have gently guided this book from inception to completion. Glen Hartley, my agent, continues to provide sage advice and direction. My assistant, Jenny Bonilla, has done much of the crafting and polishing. She has more patience and style than I do. She's also given me the opportunity to sit in the dressing room at Nordstrom and eavesdrop on shopping soap operas.

A few people agreed to walk the mall with me. To protect the innocent, they will remain nameless. Our conversations formed the basis for the dialogue constructed in this book. I thank them for their time and willingness to share.

It has been a long three years since *Why We Buy: The Science of Shopping* was published. It exists in nineteen foreign editions and has a life of its own. Here in the United States and elsewhere it continues to sell and make its way into classrooms and training programs. I have been surprised by the passionate response of readers across the globe. It has made my life both miserable and wonderful. Thank you.

It has been difficult at times, balancing the role of author with my primary job as chief executive of Envirosell. I am grateful to my colleagues who tolerate the role changes I go through. Our core group at Envirosell has worked together for more than ten years. Barbara Weisfeld, Tom Moseman, Craig Childress, and Anne Marie Luthro continue to be steadfast contributors and companions. Neither this book nor *Why We Buy* would have been possible without their support.

Every three months I go through a mantra at one of our weekly staff meetings. Envirosell is answerable to three things. First, we are answerable to our clients. They pay the bills, and their belief in us is important. Second, we are answerable to what we think is the truth. Finally, we are answerable to one another. We have no distant shareholders or management, which in the world of research and consulting makes us unique. As a small agency, we cast a remarkable shadow. We have a series of clients whose support has been critical to helping Envirosell prosper. Bob Cecil and Dave Edmondson at RadioShack, Ann Marie Stephens at Circuit City, Deborah Grassi at Wal-Mart, Francesca Schuler at the Gap, Robin Pearl at Estée Lauder, Marc Scorca at Opera America, Connie Olsen at Godiva Chocolatier, Scott Lamensdorf at Philips Lighting, and Kevin Armstrong, now at Cosi, are just a few.

Our offshore network has been particularly important. Giusi Scandroglio and Mario Scatigna in Milano, Mitsuyo Uchida in Tokyo, Kita Mastopietro and J. Augusto Domingues in São Paolo, Manolo Barberena in Mexico City, and Greg Thain in Moscow.

I have a special relationship with Japan. While it is impossible to cite all my Japanese friends, the few who follow are special. Hiroshi Hayakawa bought the Japanese rights to *Why We Buy* in spite of the fact that his imprint specializes in mystery books. I am grateful for his courage and vision. I have worked closely with Kenji Onodera at Hakuhodo, the Japanese advertising agency. I could not ask for a more responsive and dedicated colleague. Through Onodera-san's guidance and direction, Envirosell Japan has had a successful launch. Shiota-san and Asano-san at Sony Music Communication have been advisers, friends, and fine dining companions. Kazuo Nozaka is the most elegant and serene man I know. Nozaka-san is the founder of Humanold, an AARP-like service organization for Japanese seniors. His guidance, counsel, and example have been valuable to me both as a businessperson and as a man. Finally, Kaz Toyota has been my agent and friend for many years.

I have been led to and through malls across the world by Suat Soysal in Istanbul, Momo Toyota in Tokyo, Aki Toyota in Nara, George Homer and José Luis Nueno in Barcelona, John Hitcham in the United Kingdom, Peter Childs in Paris, Haakon Dahl and Christian Sinding in Oslo, Jean Pierre and Celine Baade in Strasbourg, Alberto Pasquini in Milano, and Tatiana Voronina in Moscow.

No thanks to the airline industry, I have a close network of friends working the retail and consumer-product circuit. There is rarely a place where I land that I can't find someone I'd be delighted to share a meal and opinions with: Judy Bell at Target in Minneapolis, Jim Lucas at Draft in Chicago, Lauren Askew at Monk Design in Baltimore, Carmen Spofford at the Bon in Seattle, Terry Shook and Kevin Kelley at Shook Kelley Design in Charlotte, Erika Szychowski at E°Trade in San Francisco, Karen Hyatt at Hewlett Packard in Corvallis, Bob Gorrie at Gorrie Marketing Services in Toronto, Don Whetstone at Walgreen's in Deerfield, Allen Klose at Blockbuster in Dallas, Alberto Ulloa at Coca-Cola Central American in San Jose, Costa Rica, Paul Kelly at Brown Thomas in Dublin, Patrick Lehman at Express in Columbus, David Blackwell at Ford in Detroit, Jim Ratner at Forest City in Cleveland, Ron Askew at the Integer Group in Denver, Tim Heard at the Brown Shoe Company in St. Louis, Joe Nevins at Bergmeyer in Boston, Tom Kass at Blain's Farm & Fleet in Janesville, Robert Hanson at Levi's in San Francisco, Mark Kolligian at CVS in Woonsocket, Kevin Kwiakowski at Pfizer in New Jersey, Philip Davis at Asprey in London, Mike Ernest at Sara Lee Direct in Winston-Salem, Ed Harsant at Staples in Framingham, Ken McGovern and John Menzer at Wal-Mart in Bentonville, Arnold Schmied at Silhouette in Albany, Dave Williams at Best Buy in Eden Prairie, Bobbi Brooks at RLG in Atlanta, and Jeff Williamson at the Phoenix Zoo are just a few.

It is not that in the New York metro area I have any shortage of merchant and marketer friends. Richard Marcus now lives here; our gain is Dallas's loss. Barbara Stoebel is a veteran cosmetics executive. She is always funny, insightful, and grounded. Rob Ceretti is the past president of the New York Chapter of the Institute of Store Planners and the principal at R. Ceretti & Associates. Lisa Monteleone works for Bvlgari in New York City, but serves stores across the hemisphere. Michael Gould and Jack Hruska at Bloomingdale's have facilitated our work for years. Watts Wacker, or W2 as he calls himself, lives outside the city in a place we call Connect the Dots, but I give him the benefit of the doubt. Watts is glib and inspiring. Kate Newlin reinvents her life every year or two. Anyone with the courage to adopt children after age forty deserves kudos. Wendy Liebmann is the founder of WSL Strategic Retail. She may be the most perfectly groomed person I have ever known. Richard Kurtz is one of my market research mentors. He reminds me that the spirit of life is about staying curious.

I am asked often why we, at Envirosell, continue to get good press. Envirosell had a PR agent for about ten minutes many years ago. I have no regrets about dealing directly with the media. I am happy to talk on and off the record. *New York Times, Washington Post, Los Angeles Times, Philadelphia Inquirer*: The list is endless. I am particularly grateful to the business press—*Business Week, Business 2.0, Fast Company, Fortune*, and *Fortune Small Business*, all of which have been very generous to us. I talk to *Women's Wear Daily* sometimes once a week, not bad for a fashion nerd.

Small parts of this book have appeared in DDI, the retail design trade magazine where I have a short bimonthly column. Group publisher Karen Schaffner and editor RoxAnna Sway have been generous with their time and support.

My Canadian grandmother would have been tickled pink with the attention given Envirosell and my last book by the *National Post, Toronto Globe and Mail*, the CBC, and media outlets across Canada. I think it is because the Canadians are concerned with manners, and *Why We Buy* is focused on retail manners.

A few people look out after me. They tolerate my bouts of ill temper, understand the zombie nature of jet lag, and take my late-night calls. Some of them I see often; others almost never. None of them know how important they are to me. Rip Hayman, Jeff Hewitt, Rob Hewitt, Teresa Sarno, Wilton Conner, Christine Lehner, Carol White, Hutch and Kate Raymer, Liz and Hazem Gamal, Pierre and Colleen Cournot,

Holland Williams, Michael Monroe, Lisa Underhill, Reed Valleau, Joseph Gugletti, Mitch and Mary Ann Wolf, Stan Beck, Peter and Asiye Kay, David Searles, Joe and Sandy Weishar, Joe and Jean McGuire, Sara and Jeff Bowen, John and Medora Barkley, and Mark Gillen.

My companion, who gets the best and worst of me, is Sheryl Henze. I call her Dreamboat, and she is.

A small group of us run an old 1924 forty-eight-foot yawl called the *Klang II,* which sails out of Nyack harbor. Mark, Lisa, Christine, Bill, Rip, Martin, Willie, Fred, Mike, and I meet, sail, drink, tell bad jokes, and discard stress. Their companionship has made aging a pleasure.

If this volume has urban attitude, I am merely the conduit of the training I received on and off the street. Fred Kent and Bob Cook were my early bosses at Project for Public Spaces. Harvey Flad at Vassar College and Barry Boots at Columbia University gave me my first education in Urbanism. Roberto Brambilla and Gianni Longo are two New York–based Italian architects and authors. At their Institute for Environmental Action, they exposed me to both the joy of writing about design and taught me to play and think in city scale. While Roberto has retired to develop luxury property in exotic locations, Gianni remains a remarkably effective pixie at generating sense and consensus in troubled communities across the United States. Peter Katz, the author of *The New Urbanism* is an urban policy wonk and fellow misfit, always willing to have a serious conversation at the drop of a hat. Finally is my old friend Sari Dienes, who died in 1993 at age ninety-four. She described herself as a painter, printmaker, and troublemaker. Sari was the most observant and resourceful urban person I have yet to know. Her Hungarian-accented English still sings in my ears, from our late-night citywide ramblings: "Oh, Paco, Paco, look at that!"

Index

Ortega, Amancio, 152
outdoors outfitters, 175, 194
outside appearance of malls, 19, 21

Pacific Sun, 157, 159–64, 168, 169
parking, 23–28
    for employees, 28
    finding car, 26, 213
    priorities, 24–25, 26
parking lots, 21
    innovative uses of, 26–28
percentage U.S. retailing from
        malls, 15
perfume, 64–65, 69–70, 158
pet shops, 88
piercing, 165–66
political candidates, 31–32
poor people, malls keeping out,
        34–35
Portugal, 152, 153
Prada, 148, 181
prepared-food shops, 53, 86, 105
preppy look, 159, 161–62
Prestonwood Mall, Dallas, 204
public transportation, lack of to malls,
        33, 205
pushcarts. *See* kiosks

racism, 33–34, 149
Ralph Lauren, 77, 79, 109
real estate companies' ownership of
        malls, 13–14, 19–20, 32
record stores, 158–59, 187
    lack of allure of, 133–34, 135–40
religious groups taking over failed
        malls, 204
restaurants, 15, 105
    See also food courts

Restoration Hardware, 126, 154
rest rooms. *See* bathrooms
retailing, European versus American,
        153
Roche, Daniel, 9
rock-climbing walls, 15, 69, 85, 202
Rouse Company, 97

Saks, 79
sale items:
    cosmetics, 56
    men's underwear, 49
    women's clothing, 183–84
salesclerks:
    cosmetics, 59–60
    jewelry, 117–18, 123–24
    women's clothing, 82–83
sales-per-square-foot revenues,
        148–49
Sam's Club, 116, 122
science of shopping, 7–10
Sears catalog, 10
security bag-checking, 92–94
security in malls, 112, 120–21, 145
senior citizens:
    good lighting needed for, 174
    and mall walking, 30–31
    and sneakers, 129–30
Sephora, 54, 55, 56, 152
September 11, effects on shopping,
        11–12, 92
sexuality in the mall, 61–69
shallow loop, 51
shelf/rack placement, 180–81
Sherman Oaks Galleria, Los Angeles,
        204
Shibuya Station, Tokyo, 39–41
shopping baskets, 91–92